Cycling *in*
EAST
ANGLIA

Published by Collins
An imprint of HarperCollins Publishers
77–85 Fulham Palace Road
London W6 8JB

First published 2001
© HarperCollins Publishers Ltd 2001
Maps © Bartholomew Ltd 2001

Routes compiled by Colin Kindred, Stephen Read, Bernie Seeley, Peter Whelan, Anthony Wright.
Design by Creative Matters Design Consultancy, Glasgow.
Typeset by Bob Vickers.

Photographs reproduced by kind permission of the following:
Britain on View pages 5, 8, 11, 16, 22, 23, 30, 39, 45, 47, 51, 59, 71, 74, 82, 88, 105, 110, 117;
V K Guy pages 54, 100.

Printed in Singapore

ISBN 0 00 710378 6
01/1/12

CONTENTS

KEY TO ROUTES

Route		Grade	Distance km (miles)		Time to allow	Page
1	Wickham Market and Ufford	easy	17.5	(11)	1–2 hours	14
2	Clare, Kedington and Hundon	moderate	21	(13)	2–4 hours	17
3	Hickling Broad and How Hill	easy	22.5	(14)	2–4 hours	20
4	The Sandringham Estate	moderate	24	(15)	2–4 hours	23
5	Newmarket	moderate	24	(15)	2–4 hours	26
6	Castle Acre and the Peddars Way	moderate	25.5	(16)	2–4 hours	28
7	The Wensum Valley	moderate	35.5	(22)	2–4 hours	31
8	Gressenhall and Norfolk villages	moderate	35.5	(22)	3–5 hours	35
9	Blickling and North Norfolk	moderate	37.5	(23.5)	3–5 hours	38
10	Colchester and Dedham	moderate	41.5	(26)	3–6 hours	42
11	North Norfolk – Holt and Blakeney	moderate	41.5	(26)	3–5 hours	46
12	Attleborough and Hingham	moderate	42.5	(26.5)	3–6 hours	50
13	Cambridge and Linton	moderate	46.5	(29)	3–6 hours	54
14	Woodbridge and the Deben Estuary	moderate	48	(30)	4–6 hours	58
15	Lavenham and Woolpit	moderate	48	(30)	3–6 hours	62
16	Mildenhall and Ely	moderate	48	(30)	3–6 hours	66
17	Saffron Walden and Thaxted	moderate	49.5	(31)	3–6 hours	70
18	Halesworth and Southwold	moderate	54.5	(34)	5–6 hours	74
19	Wisbech and the Fens	moderate	60	(37.5)	4–6 hours	78
20	King's Lynn and west Norfolk	moderate	75.5	(47)	4–6 hours	83
21	Thetford and Diss	moderate	78	(48.5)	4–8 hours	89
22	Norwich and Beccles	moderate	88.5	(55)	5–7 hours	95
23	Bramford, Lavenham and the Stour Valley	moderate	99.5	(62)	4–7 hours	101
24	Wells-next-the-Sea and Fakenham	strenuous	101	(63)	10–15 hours	106
25	Suffolk – a grande randonnée	strenuous	130	(81)	7–14 hours	112

Distances have been rounded up or down to the nearest 0.5km (mile).

Route colour coding

undemanding rides compiled specifically with families in mind
15–25km (10–15 miles)

middle distance rides suitable for all cyclists
25–40km (15–25 miles)

half-day rides for the more experienced and adventurous cyclist
40–60km (25–40 miles)

challenging full-day rides
over 60km (over 40 miles)

grande randonnée – a grand cycling tour
over 100km (over 60 miles)

 Routes marked with this symbol are off-road or have off-road sections
(includes well-surfaced cycleways as well as rougher off-road tracks)

Flatford Mill

LOCATION MAP

A17
A15
A16
A52
Boston
The Wash
A1
A52
24
11 Holt
Cromer
NORTH
SEA
Grantham
Sandringham 4
A148
Blickling 9
A140
A149
Hickling
3
A607
A17
King's 20
Lynn
6
Gressenhall
7
A16
A15
A16
A11(M)
A1
Castle 8
Acre
A47
Taverham
Wisbech
A47
19
A134
Norwich 22
Broads
Great
Yarmouth
A606
A606
A47
The Fens
Attleborough
A11
A146
A143
Lowestoft
A43
Peterborough
A10
12
Bungay
A146
A605
A141
A142
Thetford 21
A1066
A143
18 Halesworth
A14
Kettering
A14
Mildenhall 16
A11
A134
A12
A43
A6
A14
A142
Bury
A14
A143
A143
12
A428
5
25 St Edmunds
A140
M1
A428
Bedford
13
Newmarket
A14
Wickham
1 Market
A421
A6
Cambridge
Lavenham
Woodbridge
A5
A605
A10
M11
2
15 Ipswich
23 14
A6
A10
17 Saffron
Walden
A12
A14
Felixstowe
Milton
Keynes
A5
A1(M)
A602
A120
A131
A134
A120
10
A120
Colchester
Luton
Bishop's
Stortford
A12

KEY TO ROUTE MAPS

M23 / Service area	Motorway	Cycle route / optional route	Telephone
A259	'A' road / Dual carriageway	Start of cycle route	Picnic site
B2130	'B' road / Dual carriageway	12— Route direction	Camping site
	Good minor road	B Place of interest	Public toilets
	Minor road	Public house	Place of worship
	Track / bridleway	Café / refreshments	Viewpoint
	Railway / station	X Restaurant	Golf course
	Canal / river / lake	Convenience store	Tumulus
	Ferry route	i Tourist Information Centre	Urban area
50	Contour (height in metres)	P Parking	Woodland

Height above sea level

Land below	0	50	100	150	200	300	400	500	600	700	800 metres
sea level	0	165	330	490	655	985	1315	1645	1975	2305	2635 feet

INTRODUCTION

How to use this guide

Collins' *Cycling in East Anglia* has been devised for those who want trips out on their bicycles along quiet roads and tracks, passing interesting places and convenient refreshment stops without having to devise their own routes. Each of the 25 routes in this book has been compiled and ridden by an experienced cyclist for cyclists of all abilities.

Cycling in East Anglia is easy to use. Routes range from undemanding rides compiled specifically with families in mind to challenging full-day rides; the type of route is easily identified by colour coding (see page 5). At the start of each route an information box summarises: total distance (in kilometres/miles – distances have been rounded up or down throughout to the nearest 0.5km/mile and are approximate only); grade (easy, moderate or strenuous based on distance and difficulty); terrain; an average time to allow for the route; directions to the start of the route by car and, if appropriate, by train.

Each route is fully mapped and has concise, easy-to-follow directions. Comprehensive information on places of interest and convenient refreshment stops along each route are also given. Accumulated mileages within each route description give an indication of progress, while the profile diagram is a graphic representation of gradients along the route. These should be used as a guide only.

The following abbreviations are used in the route directions:

LHF	left hand fork
RHF	right hand fork
LHS	left hand side
RHS	right hand side
SO	straight on
SP	signpost
TJ	T junction
TL	turn left
TR	turn right
XR	crossroads

Cycling in East Anglia

This guide contains routes in Cambridgeshire, Norfolk, Suffolk and the north of Essex: from Wisbech in the west across to Hickling in the east; and from Wells-next-the-Sea in the north as far as Colchester in the south. East Anglia was settled by the Romans and the Angles. The area prospered in the Middle Ages, when the local seaports and the woollen trade were at their strongest, and was a major economic force until the early 19th-century. The industrial revolution largely passed by East Anglia, leaving the area unspoilt and with a legacy of many fine churches and medieval and Georgian buildings. Agriculture plays an important part in the economy but, in common with many areas of the country, tourism and leisure are contributing an increasing amount.

Some of the routes use sections of the National Cycle Network, which is being developed by the charity Sustrans, with the help of a £43.5 million grant from the Millennium Commission. The network will run through towns and cities and link urban areas with the countryside. In this part of the country, the network runs from Hull to Fakenham and then from Fakenham to Harwich. There are numerous cycling routes, both on- and off-road, administered by the local councils. The routes also take in two long-distance paths – the Peddars Way and the Weavers Way. For further information on the National Cycle Network write to Sustrans, 35 King Street, Bristol, BS1 4DZ, telephone (0117) 926 8893, or visit their website at www.sustrans.org.uk

Preparing for a cycling trip

Basic maintenance

A cycle ride is an immense pleasure, particularly on a warm sunny day. Nothing is better than coasting along a country lane gazing over the countryside. Unfortunately, not every cycling day is as perfect as this, and it is important to make sure that your bike is in good order and that you are taking the necessary clothing and supplies with you.

Before you go out on your bicycle check that everything is in order. Pump the tyres up if needed, and check that the brakes are working properly and that nothing is loose – the brakes are the only means of stopping quickly and safely. If there is a problem and you are not sure

River Waveney

that you can fix it, take the bike to a cycle repair shop – they can often deal with small repairs very quickly.

When you go out cycling it is important to take either a puncture repair kit or a spare inner tube – it is often quicker to replace the inner tube in the event of a puncture, though it may be a good idea to practise first. You also need a pump, and with a slow puncture the pump may be enough to get you home. To remove the tyre you need a set of tyre levers. Other basic tools are an Allen key and a spanner. Some wheels on modern bikes can be removed by quick release levers built into the bike. Take a lock for your bike and if you have to leave it at any time, leave it in public view and locked through the frame and front wheel to something secure.

What to wear and take with you

It is not necessary to buy specialised cycling clothes. If it is not warm enough to wear shorts wear trousers which are easy to move in but fairly close to the leg below the knee – leggings are ideal – as this stops the trousers catching the chain. If you haven't got narrow-legged trousers, bicycle clips will hold them in. Jeans are not a good idea as they are rather tight and difficult to cycle in, and if they get wet they take a long time to dry. If your shorts or trousers are thin you might get a bit sore from being too long on the saddle. This problem can be reduced by using a gel saddle, and by wearing thicker, or extra, pants. Once you are a committed cyclist you can buy cycling shorts; or undershorts which have a protective pad built in and which can be worn under anything. It is a good idea to wear several thin layers of clothes so that you can add or remove layers as necessary. A zip-fronted top gives easy temperature control. Make sure you have something warm and something waterproof.

If you wear shoes with a firm, flat sole you will be able to exert pressure on the pedals easily, and will have less work to do to make the bicycle move. Gloves not only keep your hands warm but protect them in the event that you come off, and cycling mittens which cushion your hands are not expensive. A helmet is not a legal requirement, but it will protect your head if you fall.

In general it is a good idea to wear bright clothing so that you can be easily seen by motorists, and this is particularly important when it is overcast or getting dark. If you might be out in the dark or twilight fit your bicycle with lights – by law your bicycle must have a reflector. You can also buy reflective bands for your ankles, or to wear over your shoulder and back, and these help motorists to see you.

You may be surprised how quickly you use up energy when cycling, and it is important to eat a carbohydrate meal before you set out. When planning a long ride, eat well the night before. You should eat small amounts of food regularly while you are cycling, or you may find that your energy suddenly disappears, particularly if there are hills or if the weather is cold. It is important to always carry something to eat with you – chocolate, bananas, biscuits – so that if you do start fading away you can restore yourself quickly. In warm weather you will sweat and use up fluid, and you always need to carry something to drink – water will do! Many bicycles have a fitment in which to put a water bottle, and if you don't have one a cycle shop should be able to fit one.

It is also a good idea to carry a small first aid kit. This should include elastoplasts or bandages, sunburn cream, and an anti-histamine in case you are stung by a passing insect.

It is a good idea to have a pannier to carry all these items. Some fit on the handlebars, some to the back of the seat and some onto a back rack. For a day's ride you probably won't need a lot of carrying capacity, but it is better to carry items in a pannier rather than in a rucksack on your back. Pack items that you are carrying carefully – loose items can be dangerous.

Getting to the start of the ride

If you are lucky you will be able to cycle to the start of the ride, but often transport is necessary. If you travel there by train, some sprinter services carry two bicycles without prior booking. Other services carry bicycles free in off-peak periods, but check the details with your local station. Alternatively, you could use your car – it may be possible to get a bike in the back of a hatchback if you take out the front wheel. There are inexpensive, easily fitted car racks which carry bicycles safely. Your local cycle store will be able to supply one to suit you.

Cycling on-road

Cycling on back roads is a delight with quiet lanes, interesting villages and good views. The cycle rides in this book are mainly on quiet roads but you sometimes cross busy roads and have stretches on A and B roads, and whatever sort of road you are on it is essential to ride safely. Always be aware of the possibility or existence of other traffic. Glance behind regularly, signal before you turn or change lane, and keep to the left. If there are motorists around, make sure that they have seen you before you cross their path. Cycling can be dangerous if you are competing for space with motor vehicles, many of which seem to have difficulty in seeing cyclists. When drivers are coming out of side roads, catch their eye before you ride in front of them.

You will find that many roads have potholes and uneven edges. They are much more difficult to spot when you are in a group because of the restricted view ahead, and therefore warnings need to be given. It is a good idea to cycle about a metre out into the road, conditions permitting, so that you avoid the worst of the uneven surfaces and to give you room to move in to the left if you are closely overtaken by a motor vehicle.

Other things to be careful of are slippery roads, particularly where there is mud or fallen leaves. Sudden rain after a period of dry weather often makes the roads extremely slippery. Dogs, too, are a hazard because they often move unpredictably, and sometimes like to chase cyclists. If you are not happy, stop or go slowly until the problem has passed.

Pedalling

Many modern bikes have 18 or 21 gears with three rings at the front and six or seven on the back wheel, and for much of the time you will find that the middle gear at the front with the range of gears at the back will be fine. Use your gears to find one that is easy to pedal along in so that your feet move round easily and you do not put too much pressure on your knees. If you are new to the bike and the gears it is a good idea to practise changing the gears on a stretch of flat, quiet road so that when you need to change gears quickly you will be ready to do so.

Cycling in a group

When cycling in a group it is essential to do so in a disciplined manner for your own, and others', safety. Do not ride too close to the bicycle in front of you – keep about a bicycle's length between you so that you will have space to brake or stop. Always keep both hands on the handlebars, except when signalling, etc. It is alright to cycle two abreast on quiet roads, but if it is necessary to change from cycling two

Blakeney Harbour

abreast to single file this is usually done by the outside rider falling in behind the nearside rider; always cycle in single file where there are double white lines, on busy roads, or on narrow and winding roads where you have a restricted view of the road ahead. Overtake on the right (outside) only; do not overtake on the inside.

It is important to pass information to other members of the group, for example:

car up – a vehicle is coming up behind the group and will be overtaking;

car down – a vehicle is coming towards the group;

single up – get into single file;

stopping – stopping, or

slowing/easy – slowing due to junction, etc., ahead;

on the left – there is an obstacle on the left, e.g. pedestrian, parked car;

pothole – pothole (and point towards it).

Accidents

In case of an accident, stay calm and, if needed, ring the emergency services on 999. It is a good idea to carry a basic first aid kit and perhaps also one of the commercial foil wraps to put around anyone who has an accident to keep them warm. If someone comes off their bicycle move them and the bike off the road if it is safe to do so. Get someone in the party to warn approaching traffic to slow down, and if necessary ring for an ambulance.

Cycling off-road

All the routes in this book take you along legal rights of way – bridleways, byways open to all traffic and roads used as public paths – it is illegal to cycle along footpaths. Generally the off-road sections of the routes will be easy if the weather and ground are dry. If the weather has been wet and the ground is muddy, it is not a good idea to cycle along bridleways unless you do not mind getting dirty and unless you have a mountain bike which will not get blocked up with mud. In dry weather any bicycle will be able to cover the bridleway sections, but you may need to dismount if the path is very uneven.

Off-road cycling is different to cycling on the road. The average speed is lower, you will use more energy, your riding style will be different and there is a different set of rules to obey – the off-road code:

1 Give way to horse riders and pedestrians, and use a bell or call out to warn someone of your presence.

2 Take your rubbish with you.

3 Do not light fires.

4 Close gates behind you.

5 Do not interfere with wildlife, plants or trees.

6 Use only tracks where you have a right of way, or where the landowner has given you permission to ride.

7 Avoid back wheel skids, which can start erosion gulleys and ruin the bridleway.

Some of the off-road rides take you some miles from shelter and civilisation – take waterproofs, plenty of food and drink and basic tools – especially spare inner tubes and tyre repair equipment. Tell someone where you are going

and approximately when you are due back. You are more likely to tumble off your bike riding off-road, so you should consider wearing a helmet and mittens with padded palms.

Useful contacts

Cycling organisations
CTC – see page 119

Sustrans – see page 8

Cycling websites
Online resources for cyclists in the UK
www.cyclecafe.com

Internet bicycling hub
www.cyclery.com

Information and support for cyclists in the UK
www.cycleweb.co.uk

Cycling information station
www.cycling.uk.com

Local cycle hire
Anglia Cycling Holidays
Sudbourne,Woodbridge
Telephone (01394) 450958

Butlers Yard
Marmora Road, Cambridge
Telephone (01223) 210420

Geoff's Bike Hire
Devonshire Road, Cambridge
Telephone (01223) 365629

Pedal Power
Tangham Forest, Woodbridge
Telephone (01473) 610500

Reepham Station
Station Road, Reepham
Telephone (01603) 871187

Local cycle shops
Anglia Bike Centre
72a Gloucester Street, Norwich
Telephone (01603) 632467

M L Walsingham & Son
Staithe Street, Wells-next-the-Sea
Telephone (01328) 710438

Tourist information
British Tourist Authority
www.visitbritain.com

East of England Tourist Board
Telephone (01473) 822922

Beccles Tourist Information Centre
Telephone (01502) 713196

Bury St Edmunds Tourist Information Centre
Telephone (01284) 764667

Cambridge Tourist Information Centre
Telephone (01223) 322640

Colchester Tourist Information Centre
Telephone (01206) 282920

Ely Tourist Information Centre
Telephone (01353) 662062

Ipswich Tourist Information Centre
Telephone (01473) 258070

King's Lynn Tourist Information Centre
Telephone (01553) 763044

Lavenham Tourist Information Centre
Telephone (01787) 248207

Newmarket Tourist Information Centre
Telephone (01638) 667200

Norwich Tourist Information Centre
Telephone (01603) 666071

Saffron Walden Tourist Information Centre
Telephone (01799) 510444

Southwold Tourist Information Centre
Telephone (01502) 724729

Wisbech Tourist Information Centre
Telephone ()1945) 583263

Woodbridge Tourist Information Centre
Telephone (01394) 382240

Sudbury Tourist Information Centre
Telephone (01787) 881320

Local councils
Breckland Council
Telephone (01362) 695333
www.breckland.gov.uk

Cambridge City Council
Telephone (01223) 457457
www.cambridge.gov.uk

Fenland District Council
Telephone (01733) 202224
www.fenland.gov.uk

Ipswich Borough Council
Telephone (01473) 432000
www.ipswich.gov.uk

Norwich City Council
Telephone (01603) 622233
www.norwich.gov.uk

St Edmundsbury Borough Council
Telephone (01284) 763233
www.stedmundsbury.gov.uk

South Norfolk Council
Telephone (01508) 533633
www.south-norfolk.gov.uk

Suffolk Coastal District Council
Telephone (01394) 383789
www.suffolkcoastal.gov.uk

Suffolk County Council
Telephone (01473) 583000
www.suffolkcc.gov.uk

Uttlesford District Council
Telephone (01799) 510510
www.uttlesford.gov.uk

Waveney District Council
Telephone (01502) 562111
www.waveney.gov.uk

King's Lynn & West Norfolk
Borough Council
Telephone (01553) 692772
www.west-norfolk.gov.uk

Other information sources for East Anglia
www.norfolkbroads.com
www.eastanglia.net
www.angliasearch.co.uk

Public transport information
UK Public Transport Information
www.pti.org.uk

National Travel Hotline
Telephone (09065) 500000

Travel by rail
National Train Enquiries Line
Telephone (08457) 484950

Railtrack
www.railtrack.com

Anglia Railways
Telephone (01473) 693333
www.angliarailways.co.uk

The Train Line
www.thetrainline.com

Virgin Trains
Telephone (08457) 222333
www.virgintrains.co.uk

Weather forecasts
BBC Weather
www.bbc.co.uk/weather

The Met. Office
Telephone 09003 406 108
www.met-office.gov.uk

UK Weather Links
www.ukweather.links.co.uk

Youth Hostels Association of England and Wales
Telephone (01727) 855215
www.yha.org.uk

WICKHAM MARKET AND UFFORD

Route information

Distance   17.5km (11 miles)

Grade   Easy

Terrain   Mostly quiet, flat roads, with just one hill.

Time to allow   1–2 hours.

Getting there by car   Campsey Ash is 3km (2 miles) east of Wickham Market on the B1078, close to the A12. Park by Wickham Market Station.

Getting there by train   Wickham Market Station is on the Ipswich–Lowestoft line. See page 13 for travel information.

This route takes in quiet lanes around the Deben Valley. From Campsey Ash you head south west through Wickham Market and on southwards to Ufford and beyond before turning north back to Campsea Ash, following pretty roads alongside the river.

Route description

Leave Wickham Market Station car park and TL onto B1078. Follow this road through Lower Hacheston, over A12 bridge to roundabout.

1   TL onto B1438, pass Hasnips cycle shop and continue into Wickham Market village square.

2   TR to visit Valley Farm.

Otherwise, SO to continue route.

3   TR into Dallinghoo Road (opposite church with spire), SP Dallinghoo 2^1/2. Take first TL into Walnut Lane. Pass church and emerge in Pettistree at TJ by church and pub.

4   TR at TJ and continue to XR (by village SP and water tower) where TL, SP Woodbridge 4/Ufford 2.

5   TR, SP Hungarian Hall.

6   TL at TJ, SP Ufford/Eyke. Continue under A12 to TJ.   *6.5km (4 miles)*

7   To visit Church of the Assumption, SO at junction.

Otherwise, TR at junction onto B1438. Continue through Ufford, past Crown pub, and LHF at junction, SP Melton.

8   TL into Old Church Road, SP Lower Ufford/Church/Eyke. Follow this winding road, past Melton Old church to TJ opposite Ufford post office.

9   TL at TJ through Lower Ufford. Continue route, arrive village SP and continue along road, SP Lougham 1^1/2.

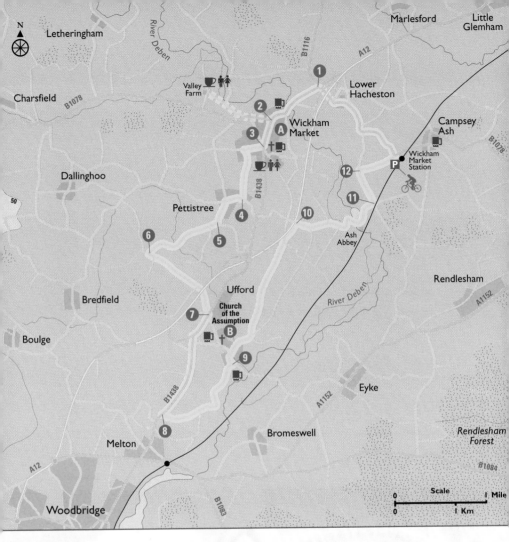

10 TR at TJ. Follow this road as it meanders past site of Ash Abbey and an old mill (private house).

11 TL at TJ by railway bridge. On left at this corner you may see sand martins flying in and out of their burrows in the sandy edges of the small cliff.

12 TR and continue to Wickham Market Station to finish the ride. **_17.5km (11 miles)_**

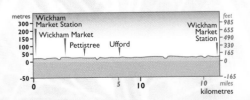

Ufford Church

Places of interest along the route

A Wickham Market

A typical small town in Suffolk, with the spired church visible from a great distance. Close by, off the B1078, is **Valley Farm Camargue Horses and White Animal Collection**, Britain's only herd of breeding Camargue horses from the south of France. Also a collection of white animals, including sheep, goats, horses, cats and dogs. Tearoom. Open all year, daily 1000–1600. Admission free (donation requested). Telephone (01728) 746916; www.valleyfarm.demon.uk

B Church of the Assumption, Ufford

The church is well-known for the large and ornately carved font cover and benches. Open all year, daily from 1000.

Food and drink

There is a pub in Campsey Ash and pubs and a tearoom in Wickham Market. Various pubs are passed en route and refreshments are available at Valley Farm.

CLARE, KEDINGTON AND HUNDON

Route information

Distance 21km (13 miles)

Grade Moderate

Terrain Mostly quiet lanes with the few climbs restricted to the middle section of the ride. There are several fast descents and children should be supervised at all times, particularly in Clare.

Time to allow 2–4 hours.

Getting there by car Clare is at the junction of the B1063 and A1092. The start of the route, Clare Castle Country Park, is signposted from the town centre and has pay and display parking.

Getting there by train There is no practical railway access to this ride.

From Clare Castle Country Park the route heads west towards the source of the River Stour: the river forms much of the boundary between Suffolk and Essex. The route initially follows narrow lanes on the Essex side to reach Stoke by Clare in Suffolk. On for a steep climb across a disused railway line to the ridge at Boyton End, for views of the River Stour and Kedington. Beyond Kedington the route goes east to Brockley Green and the highest point of the route at 112m (367.5 feet). With the major climbs over, the route descends to Chimney Street and on through Hundon and Chilton Street, with its disused windmill, back to Clare.

Places of interest along the route

A **Clare**

Clare, in west Suffolk, was recorded in the Domesday book as a settlement of extensive vineyards and 600 inhabitants. Although the vineyards are long gone, the town retains many fine timbered buildings, including the **Ancient House** in the town centre which is now the town's museum. Open Easter and May to September, Thursday, Friday and Sunday 1400–1700, Saturday and Bank Holidays 1130–1700. Charge. A market is held on Monday and Saturday. Telephone Sudbury Tourist Information Centre for more details on (01787) 881320. **Clare Castle Country Park** covers an area of 10ha (25 acres) and contains the remains of a Norman castle. The country park was also the location of Clare railway station, opened in 1865 and closed in 1967, and the goods shed now contains the park centre. Children's adventure play area, riverside and woodland walks, butterfly garden, picnic area and ranger service. Park open all year; park centre open May to September, daily; October to April at weekends and bank holidays. Telephone (01787) 277491 for information.

B **Stoke by Clare**

A sleepy rural village, set around a pleasant green. The 15th-century church contains many items of interest, including the smallest pulpit in England, dating from the 15th century and richly carved. The single-handed clock on the tower dates from around 1670. Nearby at Boyton End is **Boyton Vineyard**, offering tours and wine tastings. Also gardens and picnic area. Open April to October, daily. Admission free.

Telephone (01440) 761893 to confirm opening times.

ⓒ Kedington

Kedington is a thriving community with open green spaces and riverside walks along the River Stour. The church, **St Peter and St Paul**, is built on the site of a Roman villa and some of the Roman flooring tiles remain. Although the core of the church dates from the 14th century, the interior has been unchanged for the past 250 years, making its boxed pews and splendid interior fittings unique in Suffolk. Open Easter to September, weekends and bank holidays 1400–1600. Outside of these times, the keys are available from the post office (TL from church then TR and TL into Westward Deals).

Route description

From Clare Castle Country Park car park TR into Maltings Lane (to pass Antiques World).

1 TL into Nethergate Street (A1092), towards Haverhill.

2 TL, SP Ashen, and cross River Stour.

3 SO and follow road to right, SP Ashen.

4 SO, SP Ashen. Continue as lane becomes single track as far as outskirts of Stoke by Clare.

5 TR, SP Stoke.

6 SO, past Doctors Lane on LHS.

7 TR, SP Stoke. Cross River Stour and continue into village.

8 TL at TJ onto A1092, SP Wixoe (opposite Lion pub). *4.5km (3 miles)*

9 TR into Blacksmiths Hill, for a short steep climb to cross disused railway. Continue for gradual climb.

10 Take LHF and follow lane down (Farmers Farm visible above on RHS).

11 Take LHF to pass Burnt House Farm and entrance to Stonards Farm. CARE – fast

descent along single track road with loose surface. Continue and climb up switchback to Boyton End.

12 To visit Boyton Vineyard, TL at TJ.

Otherwise, TR at TJ then take LHF to pass Boyton Hall on RHS (8km/5 miles). Continue for easy climb to ridge overlooking River Stour, then long descent to outskirts of Kedington.

13 Continue SO, past Simm's Lane on RHS and several estate roads.

14 To visit village store, post office and pub, TL at TJ.

Otherwise, to continue route, TR at TJ, SP Hundon.

15 To visit Kedington church, TL at TJ for approximately 200m. Otherwise, TR at TJ, SP Hundon 2 and continue SO, past Dash End Lane on LHS, as road slowly climbs to Brockley Green.

16 Arrive Brockley Green. Continue SO, past Simm's Lane on RHS. Pass Plough Country Hotel and take LHF, SP Steeple Chase. Follow single track lane for gentle climb to pass highest point of the ride – a redundant triangulation pillar at 112m (367.5 feet).

17 Arrive Chimney Street and continue SO, past byroad on RHS.

18 TR at TJ into Barnardiston Road, then RHF, SP Hundon.

19 LHF, SP Stradishall, for gentle climb towards Hundon. Continue SO, passing minor roads on LHS and RHS, to arrive facing Hundon village church.

20 TR at TJ and descend past Rose & Crown pub on LHS, village SP and war memorial.

21 TL at TJ into Clare Road, SP Clare. The route now gently descends towards Clare.

22 SO, SP Clare (ignore both lanes joining from RHS before and after bend).
16.5km (10.5 miles)

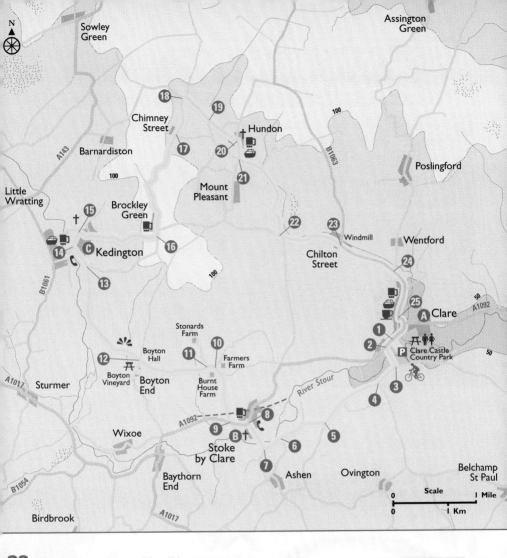

23 Arrive Chilton Street. SO at TJ onto B1063, SP Clare. Continue, past disused tower windmill on LHS.

24 Continue SO as Clare Road joins from LHS, SP Clare. Stay on B1063 (becomes Callis Street).

25 Take LHF (B1063) into Church Street, SP Haverhill/Sudbury. Then SO at TJ, SP Haverhill/B1092, and pass Clare's Market Hill on RHS. Continue SO into Well Lane (A1092). TL into The Broadway, SP Clare Castle Country Park, and TL into car park to finish the ride.

21km (13 miles)

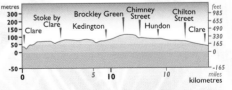

Food and drink

Plenty of choice in Clare. Bar meals are available at the pubs passed en route.

HICKLING BROAD AND HOW HILL

Route information

 Distance   22.5 km (14 miles)

Grade   Easy

Terrain   Quiet country roads and a section of bridleway

Time to allow   2–4 hours.

Getting there by car   Hickling Broad is approximately 16km (10 miles) north west of Great Yarmouth.

Getting there by train   There is no convenient railway access to this route.

A route through the Norfolk Broads starting from Hickling Broad and making a circuit via Potter Heigham, Ludham and Catfield.

Route description

TL from Hickling Broad car park into Staithe Road.

1   TL at XR into Heath Road, SP Potter Heigham. Continue and SO at XR, SP Potter Heigham.

2   TL, SP Byroad. Continue and SO at XR into Green Lane, SP Potter Heigham.

3   TL into Church Lane.

4   Continue SO, staying on bridleway. Then RHF into Church Lane (becomes School Road) towards centre of Potter Heigham. SO, passing Dove House Lane on LHS and continue into village.

5   SO, SP No Through Road. SO at XR, across A149 into Byroad. Pass Fritton House on LHS.

6   TL at XR, SP Ludham. Pass Malthouse farmhouse on RHS. Take RHF towards Ludham.

7   SO at XR into School Road, SP How Hill (8km/5 miles). Ludham village on LHS. Continue SO, passing several lanes in quick succession.

8   TR, SP How Hill. Continue and pass entrance to How Hill Nature Reserve on LHS. Climb and descend How Hill.

9   RHF, past Grove Farm Studio/Gallery. Continue SO, past Waterpiece Lane on RHS.

10   TL at TJ, SP Catfield. Pass Elderbush Lane then Mill Lane on RHS.

11   TL into Church Road, SP Church/School. Continue SO, SP Fenside. Pass church and war memorial and SO into Lodge Road.

12   SO at XR, SP Stalham. Follow lane as it bears right.

13   TL at TJ towards A149, SP Sutton (16km/10 miles). SO at XR (across A149) into Old Yarmouth Road, SP Sutton. Continue towards Sutton.

14   SO, SP Stalham. Pass Methodist Chapel and continue SO, SP Stalham, into Sutton. (Staithe Road and Sutton Staithe Inn & Restaurant on LHS.)

15   TR into Rectory Road, SP Hickling.

16   TR at TJ into Church Road, SP Hickling Broad. Continue SO between church and cottages.

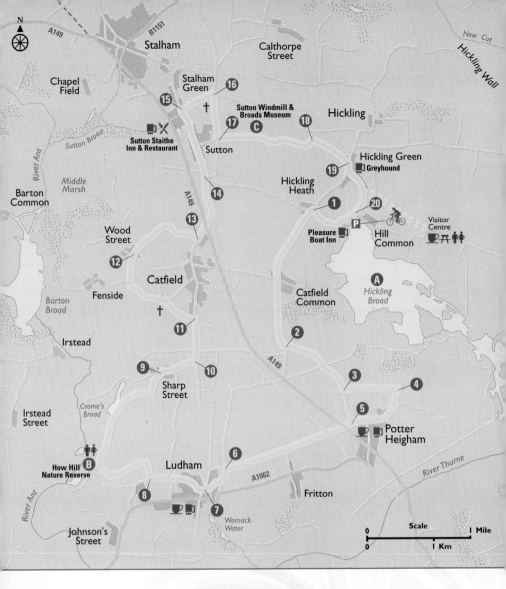

17　TL into Mill Lane. SO and pass Sutton Windmill & Broads Museum on LHS.

18　TR (lane can be muddy) and continue into Hickling Green.

19　TR at TJ towards The Green. Take LHF into Ouse Lane. Pass Greyhound pub then Stubb Lane on LHS (TL here to visit Hickling Broad visitor centre), Mill Close and Mallard Way on RHS.

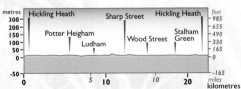

20　SO into Staithe Road. Pass Hill Common on LHS. Then moorings on Hickling Broad. TL into car park to finish the ride.

22.5km (14 miles)

Ⓐ Hickling Broad

The Norfolk Broads are a series of shallow lakes, generally surrounded by reedy marshes. The area is full of wildlife and was designated a National Park in 1988. Hickling Broad is the largest and most northerly of the broads and popular with sailors and windsurfers. It is managed by the Norfolk Wildlife Trust and is an important site for migrant birds. Free access at all reasonable times. The trust has a visitor centre just to the north of Hickling Broad. There is a boardwalk trail and bird watching hides. Picnic area. Refreshments available. Open April to September, daily 1000–1700. Charge. Telephone (01692) 598276.

Ⓑ How Hill Nature Reserve, How Hill

The nature reserve comprises marsh meadows, dykes , woodland, open water and stretches of reed and sedge beds which are managed in the traditional way. There are footpaths and nature trails and a water trail onboard an electric boat. Also on the estate is Toad Hole Cottage, once the home of the local marshman. Today it contains an information centre and a museum depicting the life of a marshman 100 years ago. Walks open April, May and October, daily 1100–1700; June to September, daily 1000–1800. Charge. Water trail open April, May and October, weekends 1100–1700 (book in advance); June to September, daily 1000–1700. Charge. Toad Hole Cottage open April, May and October, Monday–Saturday 1100–1700; June to September, daily 1000–1800. Admission free. Telephone (01692) 678763.

Ⓒ Sutton Windmill and Broads Museum, Sutton

The drainage mills are an important feature of the broads landscape. In the 19th century there were over 240 mills but today only around 70 survive. Sutton Mill has nine floors, one of the tallest surviving mills. It was constructed in 1789 and was in use until 1940. On a clear day visitors can see for miles from the top gallery. The museum describes the local history with a huge display of objects. Open April to September, daily 1000–1730. Charge. Telephone (01692) 581195.

For more information on the Norfolk Broads visit www.broads.co.uk

Hickling Broad

Food and drink

Refreshments are available in Potter Heigham and Ludham.

🛏 **Pleasure Boat Inn, Hickling Broad**
Meals served daily.

🛏 **Sutton Staithe Inn & Restaurant, Sutton Staithe**
Pub, restaurant and riverside picnic area. Note: cyclists will have to cross the A149 to reach this pub.

THE SANDRINGHAM ESTATE

Route information

Distance 24km (15 miles)

Grade Moderate

Terrain Minor roads with two short but steep climbs, and gently undulating single track lanes. The route follows a section of the National Cycle Network (NCR 1).

Time to allow 2–4 hours.

Getting there by car Sandringham is 11km (7 miles) north east of King's Lynn, reached from the A149 and A148. Park in the car park by the visitor centre, the start of the route.

Getting there by train The nearest railway station is at King's Lynn. Although the roads between King's Lynn and Sandringham are busy, NCR 1 runs between the two locations. For more information and a map of the route, contact Sustrans (see page 8) or King's Lynn Tourist Information Centre (see page 13).

This route takes you around Sandringham, the country retreat of HM The Queen and HRH The Duke of Edinburgh. From the visitor centre, the route heads west to Wolferton and then turns east and climbs through West Newton to Anmer. On north west to Shernborne and Ingoldisthorpe before returning to the visitor centre.

Places of interest along the route

A **Sandringham Estate**

Sandringham was built by King Edward VII and passed down through three generations of monarchs as a private home. The **house** contains family portraits, porcelain, jade, crystal and silver, as well as much else. Open mid-April to mid-July and August to October, daily 1100–1645. The **museum** is housed in the old coach and stable block and has displays on Royal life and the history of the estate. Open mid-April to mid-July and August to September, daily 1100–1700; October weekends only 1030–1600. The **grounds** cover 24ha (60 acres) planted with trees, shrubs and flowers. Also lakes, a stream and a waterfall. Open mid-April to mid-July, August and October, daily 1030–1700. The **country park** comprises 243ha (600 acres) of woodland and heath with visitor centre (including tearoom and restaurant), nature trails and quiet places for a picnic. Open April to October, daily 1030–1700. There is an admission charge for the house, museum and grounds. Admission is free to the country park and visitor centre. For more information telephone (01553) 772675.

B **Dersingham Nature Reserve, near Sandringham**

Managed by English Nature, the reserve has three distinct habitats – waterlogged mire, heath and woodland. The best time to visit is during July and August. Woodland walk and view point. Free access at all reasonable times. Telephone (01603) 620558 for more information.

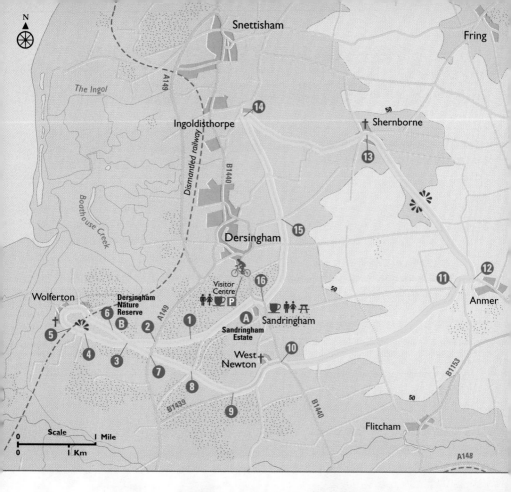

Map labels: Snettisham, Fring, The Ingol, A149, Ingoldisthorpe, ⑭, ⑬ † Shernborne, 50, B1440, Dismantled railway, Boathouse Creek, ⑮, Dersingham, ⑪ ⑫, Anmer, Wolferton, Dersingham Nature Reserve, ⑥ ⑧ Visitor Centre, ⑯, 50, ⑤ ⑥ ⑧ ②, ①, Ⓐ Sandringham, Sandringham Estate, ④ ③ ⑦, ⑧, West Newton, ⑩, B1153, ⑨, B1439, B1440, 50, Flitcham, Scale, 1 Mile, 1 Km, A148

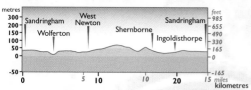

Elevation profile: metres 300, 200, 150, 100, 50, 0, -50 — Sandringham, Wolferton, West Newton, Shernborne, Sandringham, Ingoldisthorpe — feet 985, 655, 490, 330, 165, 0, -165 — 0, 5, 10, 15 miles / 10, 20 kilometres

Route description

Start with your back to the visitor centre tearoom and follow path to road. TR towards A149 and join NCR 1. Then take RHF, leaving NCR 1.

1 SO, passing scenic drive on RHS (worth visiting when rhododendrons are in flower).

2 SO across A149 at staggered XR, SP Wolferton.

3 SO at XR.

4 SO at XR. Good views of coast on RHS. Descend into Wolferton.

5 SO, past church on LHS, social club on RHS then former railway station (now private houses) on LHS. Ignore lane on RHS and continue SO for climb.

6 Near summit of climb pass access to Dersingham Nature Reserve. Continue and SO at XR.

7 SO at XR with A149.

8 SO at XR (crossing NCR 1).

9 TL at TJ onto B1439 towards West Newton. Continue SO past West Newton village SP (8km/5 miles) and past social club and church, lane on LHS and post office.

10 SO at staggered XR with B1440, towards ornate water tower on hill (this is the last climb). SO at crest of hill, past lane on RHS. Continue SO towards Anmer.

11 SO as lanes join from LHS and RHS. Descend to XR.

12 TL at XR, SP Shernborne. Continue SO along lane to Sherborne (good views) to arrive at complicated TJ overlooked by church.

13 TL at TJ, SP Dersingham. Almost immediately TR, SP Ingoldisthorpe (16.5km/ 10.5 miles). Continue into Ingoldisthorpe.

14 TL at TJ into Chalk Pit Road, rejoining NCR 1. Continue SO, past lane on RHS.

15 SO at XR, SP NCR 1. Then SO at XR on descent. Pass school on RHS. Continue for gentle climb past saw mill on LHS.

16 TR at TJ onto B1440, SP NCR 1. Then TL, SP Sandringham/NCR 1. Continue past Norwich Gates and car park entrance. TR and follow path back to visitor centre to complete the ride.

24km (15 miles)

Food and drink

The only opportunity for refreshment is at the visitor centre. Cyclists may wish to carry food and drink with them.

Sandringham Estate

NEWMARKET

Route information

Distance 24km (15 miles)

Grade Moderate

Terrain Mostly quiet, flat roads.

Time to allow 2–4 hours.

Getting there by car Newmarket is 21km (13 miles) east of Cambridge on the A142 and A1304. There are several car parks in the town, including one at the railway station, the start of the ride.

Getting there by train There are regular services to Newmarket Station. See page 13 for travel information.

The route circuits the countryside east of Newmarket, passing through Moulton, site of a medieval pack horse bridge, Dalham and Cheveley.

Places of interest along the route

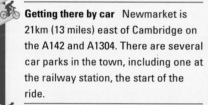

A Newmarket

Newmarket is a thriving market town, head-quarters of British horse racing. The sport grew under the Royal patronage of Kings James I and his grandson Charles II. The first recorded race at Newmarket took place in 1622. The **National Stud** offers guided tours to see the breeding mares and their foals. Open March to September, Monday–Saturday 1115 and 1430, Sunday 1430. Charge. Telephone (01638)

666789. The **National Horse Racing Museum** features an exhibition exploring the relationship between people and horses. Also tours of a training yard. Café. Open Easter to October, Tuesday–Saturday and Bank Holiday Mondays 1000–1700. Charge. Telephone (01638) 667333. For more information on Newmarket visit www.newmarket-suffolk.com

Route description

Leave Newmarket Station and TR into Green Road. SO at next three XR (Green Road becomes Granby Street, then Vicarage Road) until arrive at TJ where TL into Old Station Road.

1 TR, SP Moulton. Follow this road, gently climbing into open countryside towards Moulton.

2 SO at XR into Bridge Street. SO across River Kennet, passing pack horse bridge on LHS. Join Gazeley Road and continue climbing.

3 TR at TJ into The Street, SP Dalham. Continue SO, SP Dalham, passing Chequers pub. *9km (5.5 miles)*

4 LHF, SP Dalham. Descend through wood, SO at XR, and continue into Dalham, as far as river.

5 SO at TJ, onto B1085. Continue SO, SP Lidgate.

6 TR at XR onto B1063, SP Newmarket, for gentle climb (just before next junction, in thicket on RHS, are ruins of an ancient church).

7 LHF, SP Upend. Then RHF, SP Cheveley. *16km (10 miles)*

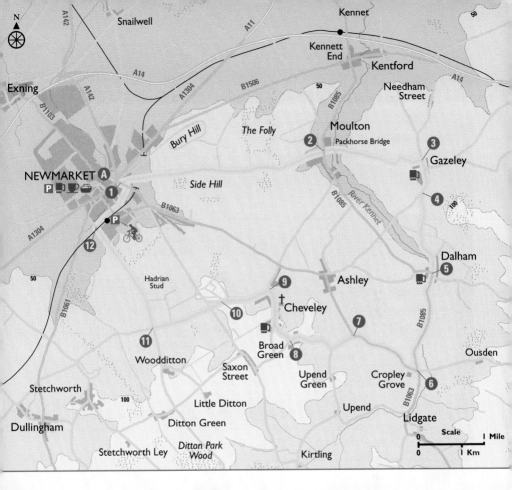

8 TR into Coach Lane, SP Cheveley. Continue to TJ (facing Red Lion pub) and TR, SP Newmarket. Continue SO, passing lane on LHS, church and lane on RHS.

9 TL into Park Road, SP Stetchworth.

10 LHF, SP Stetchworth, for descent to XR, where SO across Duchess Drive.

11 TR at TJ, SP Newmarket. Continue along this road as it descends, climbs and descends again, passing Derisley Wood and Hadrian Stud on RHS. Cross humped railway bridge.

12 Immediately TR into Paddock Drive. Continue and TR into station car park to finish the ride. ***24km (15 miles)***

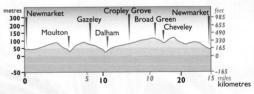

Food and drink

Plenty of choice in Newmarket. Several pubs are passed along the route.

6

CASTLE ACRE AND THE PEDDARS WAY

Route information

 Distance   25.5km (16 miles)

Grade   Moderate

Terrain   Quiet, generally flat country lanes.

Time to allow   2–4 hours.

Getting there by car   Castle Acre is in west Norfolk, approximately 6.5km (4 miles) north east of Swaffham, just west of the A1065. There is car parking by Stock Green in the centre of the village, by the castle and at the priory, the start of the ride (this car park is open only when the priory is open.

Getting there by train   There is no practical railway access to this route.

From the village of Castle Acre the route heads north and then east to Great Massingham. From here the route returns to Castle Acre, following a short section of the Peddars Way, an ancient route thought to have been in use before the Romans constructed the way after 61 AD.

Route description

Leave priory car park and TR into Priory Road, SP Castle. Continue SO through village, passing Little Lane on LHS, then South Acre Road, St James Church and Stock Green on RHS. SO at TJ, passing bailey (castle) gate on RHS.

1   TR into Pye's Lane, SP Castle, and descend, passing castle remains on RHS.

Continue along lane, to pass castle car park and De Warenne Place on RHS. SO at staggered XR.

2   TL at TJ into North Street. TR at St James Green into Orchard Lane. Then, SO at XR, SP Rougham. Continue along narrow, gently undulating lane.

3   SO, ignoring TR to Lodge Farm.

4   SO at XR, and follow lane as it bears left.

5   SO at staggered XR, SP Rougham.

6   TL at TJ, SP Weasenham (5.5km/3.5 miles). Continue through Rougham, ignoring TL to Kings Lynn and following road as it turns right.

7   TL, SP Massingham.

8   TL at XR, SP Massingham (8km/5 miles). Continue SO into Great Massingham, to pass school and pond.

9   To visit Rose and Crown pub, RHF.

To continue route, LHF into Castle Acre Road.

10   TR into Drunken Drove.

11   TL at XR, SP Peddars Way.
12.5km (8 miles)

12   Arrive XR with B1145 and SO, SP Peddars Way. Then LHF, following Peddars Way uphill and continue SO.

13   TR at XR, leaving Peddars Way (which continues to Castle Acre).

14   TL at XR, SP West Acre Gardens.
16km (10 miles)

15   To visit West Acre Gardens, TL at XR.

Or, SO to continue route.

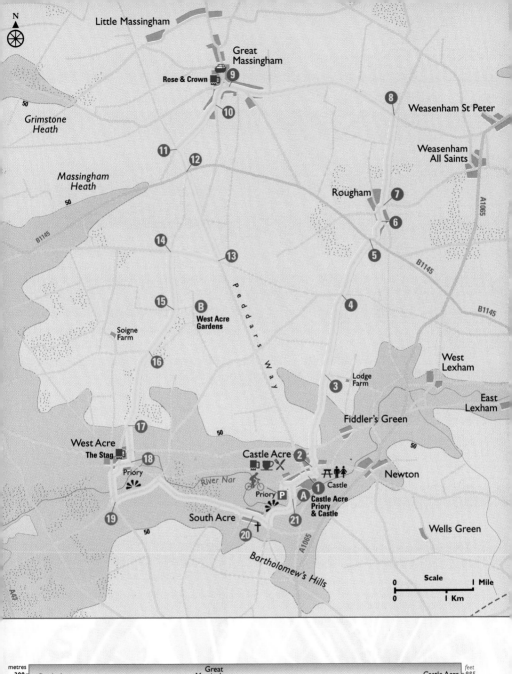

N

Little Massingham

Great Massingham

Rose & Crown ⑨

⑩

⑧ Weasenham St Peter

Grimstone Heath

50

⑪

⑫

Weasenham All Saints

Massingham Heath

50

B1145

Rougham ⑦

⑥

A1065

⑭

⑬

⑤

B1145

⑮

Ⓑ
West Acre Gardens

Peddars Way

⑯

Soigne Farm

B1145

West Lexham

③ Lodge Farm

East Lexham

⑰

Fiddler's Green

50

West Acre

The Stag

⑱

② Castle Acre

Newton

Priory

River Nar

Priory

P

① Castle

Ⓐ Castle Acre Priory & Castle

⑲

South Acre

50

⑳ †

㉑

Wells Green

Bartholomew's Hills

A1065

Scale

0   1 Mile
0   1 Km

A47

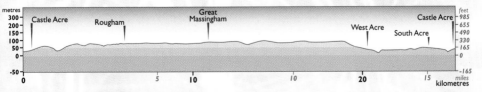

metres
300
200
150
100
50
0
-50

Castle Acre

Rougham

Great Massingham

West Acre

South Acre

Castle Acre

feet
985
655
490
330
165
0
-165

0   5   10   15
kilometres

miles

Castle Acre Priory

(views of priory on LHS). Dismount and cross river via footbridge.

21 SO, passing Blind Lane and Chimney Street on RHS. Continue uphill towards church. TL at TJ into Priory Lane. TL, SP Priory, and finish the ride in the car park.

25.5km (16 miles)

Places of interest along the route

A Castle Acre Priory and Castle, Castle Acre
The castle and priory were founded soon after the Norman conquest of 1066. Today visitors can enjoy the peaceful location, extensive earthworks and superb Norman remains. Also modern herb garden. Picnic areas. English Heritage property. Priory open April to October, daily 1000–1800; November to March, Wednesday–Sunday 1000–1600. Charge. Free access to castle at all reasonable times. Telephone (01760) 755394; www.english-heritage.org.uk

B West Acre Gardens, West Acre
Set within an old walled garden, there are extensive display gardens and a sales area containing a large range of different plants. Open February to November, daily 1000–1700. Admission free. Telephone (01760) 755562.

16 SO at staggered XR, passing TR to Soigne Farm.

17 Take LHF. SO at XR into Low Road and continue into West Acre.

18 RHF, passing The Stag pub, All Saints church and entrance to priory ruins (private). TL at XR and pass village hall on RHS. TL at TJ.

19 TL, SP South Acre. Continue for views on LHS of ruins of West Acre Priory and the Nar Valley. Take RHF (LHF SP Ford Unsuitable for Vehicles) and continue along this road.

20 SO, passing isolated church (24km/15 miles). TL at XR, SP Ford Unsuitable for Vehicles), and rejoin Peddars Way. Continue along lane as it descends towards River Nar

Food and drink

Castle Acre has a tearoom, pub and restaurant. There is a post office and convenience store in Great Massingham.

Rose & Crown, Great Massingham
Bar meals served.

The Stag, West Acre
Food available.

THE WENSUM VALLEY

Route information

Distance 35.5km (22 miles)

Grade Moderate

Terrain Well-surfaced cycle track and quiet, gently undulating lanes. The route follows sections of the Marriott's Way (MW), a traffic-free route for cyclists, walkers and horse riders (part of the National Cycle Network/NCR 1).

Time to allow 2–4 hours.

Getting there by car The route starts from the Fir Covert Road car park at Freeland Corner (between the villages of Felthorpe and Taverham), just north west of Drayton. Drayton is a suburb of Norwich, 8km (5 miles) north west of the town centre on the A1067. Alternatively, park in the centre of Drayton and start the route on the MW in Drayton (at XR with A1067).

Getting there by train The nearest railway station is in Norwich. NCR 1 and the MW run between Norwich and the start of the route at Freeland Corner. Contact the Tourist Information Centre or Norwich City Council (see page 13) for a Norwich Cycle Routes Map.

The route starts near Drayton and follows the Marriott's Way north west to Blackwater, on the northern side of the River Wensum, the elevated sections of the path providing pleasant

views. From here the route follows a series of quiet country lanes, through Sparham, across the river and on through Lyng and Ringland, which all have interesting old churches. The route continues through Drayton and back to the Marriott's Way car park to complete the circuit.

Places of interest along the route

Ⓐ Marriott's Way

This traffic-free path has been constructed along the line of the disused railway line between Themelthorpe and Norwich, originally constructed between 1882 and 1883. The lines were never particularly profitable, carrying mostly freight, but they remained open until 1985. The route is named after William Marriott, the chief engineer and manager of the railway company for 41 years. There are car parks at regular intervals along the route. Contact Norwich City Council or the Tourist Information Centre for more details (see page 13).

Ⓑ Lost World Dinosaur Park, Lenwade

A short distance from the Marriott's Way, the park contains life size models of dinosaurs in a woodland setting. Also maze, children's play areas and picnic areas. Refreshments available. Open daily, March to September 1000–1700; October 1000–1600. Charge. Telephone to confirm times on (01603) 870245; www.dinosaurpark.co.uk

Ⓒ Sparham Pools, Lyng

Partly flooded gravel pits, with reed beds, islands, scrub and mature trees. Free access to path around reserve at all times. Administered

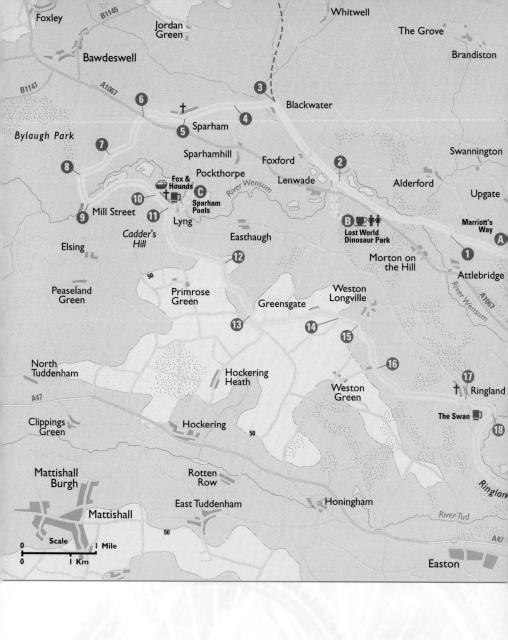
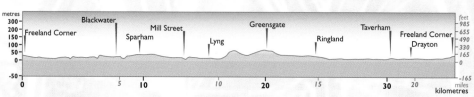

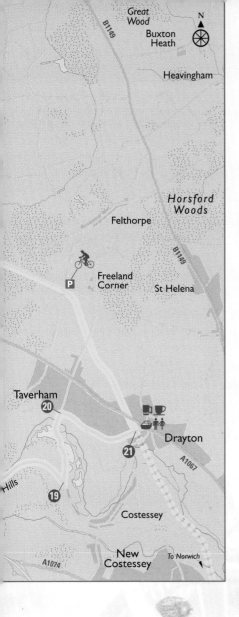

by the Norfolk Wildlife Trust. Telephone (01603) 625540; www.wildlifetrust.org.uk

There is plenty of interest in Norwich. If you start this route from the city, contact the Tourist Information Centre (see page 13) for information.

Route description

TR out of Fir Covert Road car park and immediately TR to join MW/NCR 1, SP Reepham. Continue along MW/NCR 1 as it crosses service road to Attlebridge Quarry and goes beneath road bridge.

1 TR at TJ, SP NCR 1, and join Station Road. Then TL, SP NCR 1. Continue along NCR 1, across River Wensum, service road to industrial complex and past Lenwade's redundant railway station and platform.

2 To visit Lost World Dinosaur Park, TL off NCR 1, SO at XR with A1067 (CARE) and follow SP to park

Otherwise, to continue route, continue SO along NCR 1, past car park, across tributary of River Wensum and past road bridge just outside Blackwater.

3 Immediately beyond road bridge (8km/ 5 miles), TR, dismount and ascend steps to road where remount and TR.

4 SO at XR, SP Sparham, and continue into village.

5 TR at TJ, SP Bawdeswell, joining Well Lane. Stay on Well Lane, past St Mary's Church, to XR with A1067.

6 SO at XR, SP Bylaugh.

7 SO, SP Bylaugh.

8 TL at XR, SP Lyng. Follow lane as it descends across River Wensum.

9 TL at TJ, SP Lyng. Then continue SO, SP Sparham, joining The Common (road name).

10 SO (The Common becomes The Street). Pass post office and stores on LHS, then Fox and Hounds pub and St Margaret's Church.

11 To visit Sparham Pools, TL.

Otherwise, TR, SP Hockering, and climb Cadder's Hill. Continue SO, following SP Elsing (16km/10 miles), then SP Weston Longville.

12 RHF, SP Weston Longville.

13 SO along Collins Green Lane. TL at TJ and continue SO towards Weston Longville.

14 SO, SP Weston Longville, joining Rectory Road.

15 TR at TJ, SP Hockering. Then TL, SP Ringland.

16 SO, SP Ringland, and follow lane down past St Peter's Church and lane on RHS.

17 SO at XR towards village centre, passing Ringland village SP. *25km (15.5 miles)*

18 TR at TJ, SP Costessey. Pass The Swan pub and continue SO, SP Costessey. Pass entrance to Costessey Quarry on RHS.

19 TL, SP Taverham.

20 To visit Sparham Pools, TL at XR and continue for short distance.

Otherwise, TR at XR, SP Drayton, for gentle climb towards Drayton. Pass Station Road on RHS and:

20 TL, SP NCR 1/Reepham (32km/20 miles). SO at XR with A1067 (use crossing) and again SO at XR, SP NCR 1. Cross village green and pass under road. TR at XR into Fir Covert Road and TL into car park to finish the ride.

35.5km (22 miles)

Food and drink

Refreshments are available in Drayton and at the Lost World Dinosaur Park.

Fox & Hounds, Lyng
Well-known for the weekly jazz sessions. The pubs serves real ale and good food.

The Swan, Ringland
Food available.

River view

GRESSENHALL AND NORFOLK VILLAGES

This route circuits the countryside to the west of Gressenhall, initially heading north to Whissonsett before turning south through Tittleshall and Litcham and back to Gressenhall.

Route information

Distance   35.5km (22 miles)

Grade   Moderate

Terrain   Quiet, minor roads.

Time to allow   3–5 hours.

Getting there by car   Gressenhall is 3km (2 miles) north west of East Dereham, off the B1146. The start of the route, the Norfolk Rural Life Museum, is signposted from the village. Parking is free of charge.

Getting there by train   There is no practical railway access to this ride.

Places of interest along the route

A **Norfolk Rural Life Museum and Union Farm, Gressenhall**

The museum complex occupies the site of the Mitford and Launditch Union Workhouse, built in 1776. The museum describes Norfolk's rural history and there are recreated workshops, including a saddlery and a wheelwright. Also bakery, village shop and farm worker's cottage. Union Farm is worked with horses and stocks

Clare (see Route 2)

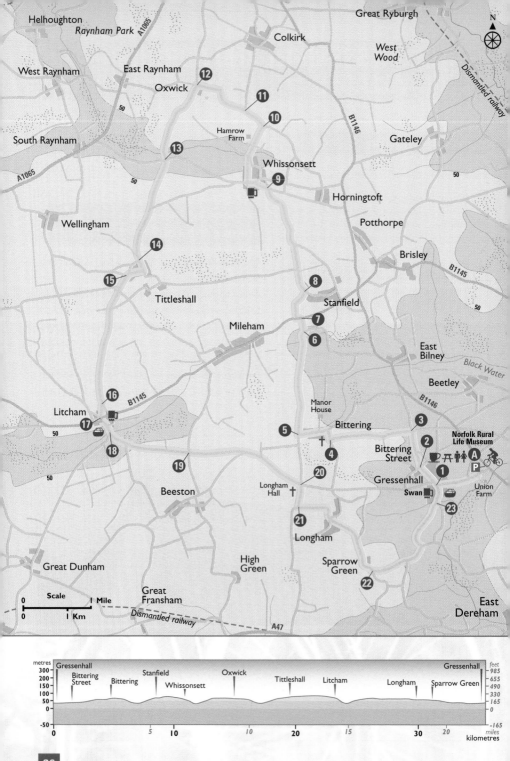

rare breeds of sheep, pigs and cattle. Café, picnic area, woodland and riverside walks. Open April to October, daily 1000–1700. Charge. Telephone (01362) 860563.

Route description

Leave the museum car park, following exit SP to lane, and TR towards Gressenhall. Continue SO, passing museum entrance on RHS and Union Farm on LHS, and into village, facing Swan pub.

1 TR at staggered XR into Bittering Street, SP Bilney.

2 SO at XR, SP East Bilney. Pass Methodist Chapel on LHS and Chequers Lane on RHS.

3 TL at XR. Continue SO, passing bridleway on LHS.

4 TR at TJ. Then LHF towards church. Pass church entrance and Manor Farm.

5 TR at TJ.

6 LHF, SP Mileham.

7 SO at staggered XR, SP Whissonsett.
8km (5 miles)

8 LHF, SP Tittleshall. Continue SO, following SP Whissonsett.

9 TL at TJ and continue through Whissonsett. Take LHF, pass post office and church on RHS. TR at XR into London Road, SP Colkirk. Continue along this road, SP Colkirk, passing entrance to Hamrow Farm.

10 LHF, SP Colkirk.

11 TL, SP Oxwick.

12 TL at TJ, SP Tittleshall.

13 SO at XR (Pear Tree Corner), SP Tittleshall (16.5km/10.5 miles). Continue along this road, following SP Tittleshall.

14 LHF into Church Lane, SP Stanfield. Pass village green and church on LHS. TR into High Street, SP Weasenham. Continue along this road, passing village hall and Methodist chapel on RHS.

15 TL at TJ then SO at XR. Continue SO, SP Litcham, past war memorial on RHS, lane on LHS.

16 RHF and continue into Litcham.

17 LHF then SO at XR, across B1145. Continue SO, past church, post office and stores on RHS, then Druids Lane on LHS.

18 LHF, SP Beeston. Continue SO, past Watery Lane on RHS.   *24km (15 miles)*

19 SO at XR, SP Longham. Then continue SO, SP Gressenhall, past entrance to Bell Hall.

20 TR at XR, SP Wendling 3. Continue SO, past entrance to Longham Hall then church.

21 LHF, SP Longham. Continue to XR where SO, SP Scaling.

22 TL, SP Gressenhall (31.5km/19.5 miles). Continue SO into Gressenhall.

23 TL at TJ into Bridge Street, SP Beeston. TR at staggered XR, SP Rural Life Museum, retrace route to museum and TL into car park to finish the ride.   *35.5km (22 miles)*

Food and drink

Refreshments are available at the museum. There are several pubs and convenience stores en route.

BLICKLING AND NORTH NORFOLK

Route information

Distance 37.5km (23.5 miles)

Grade Moderate

Terrain Gently undulating, single track lanes.

Time to allow 3–5 hours.

Getting there by car Blickling Hall is 2.5km (1.5 miles) north west of Aylesham on the B1345. It is well signposted and there is plenty of parking (free of charge).

Getting there by train There is no practical railway access to this ride.

A circuit through rural north Norfolk. From Blickling Hall the route heads north to join the Weavers Way, a long distance path linking the Norfolk Coast Path at Cromer with Great Yarmouth. Gresham is the most northerly point of the route and from here you turn south back to Blickling Hall. The route passes through pretty villages with interesting churches.

Places of interest along the route

A Blickling Hall, Blickling

The house was built in the early 17th century and contains fine collections of furniture, pictures and tapestries. The surrounding gardens and parkland provide beautiful walks. Also countryside and RAF exhibition. National Trust property. Shop, plant centre, bookshop and restaurant. House open April to October, Wednesday–Sunday 1300–1630. Garden open as per house and also November to March, Thursday–Sunday 1100–1600. Park and woods open all year, daily dawn to dusk. Charge. Telephone (01263) 738030; www.nationaltrust.org.uk

B Mannington Hall, near Aylsham

Mannington Hall is a 15th-century moated house. The surrounding gardens feature roses and wildflowers, and there are countryside walks through the parkland. Walks open all year, daily 0900–dusk. Gardens open May to September, Sunday 1200–1700; June to August also Wednesday–Friday 1100–1700. Hall open on selected days during the year. Charge. Telephone (01263) 584175.

Food and drink

Refreshments are available at Blicking Hall and Mannington Hall. Several pubs are passed along the route and there is a convenience store in Corpusty.

Route description

From Blickling Hall car park, follow SP to exit and TL onto B1345 toward Aylsham. Continue SO, SP Aylsham. Pass St Andrews Church on LHS.

1 TL, SP Ingworth. Continue SO this road, following SP Ingworth.

Blickling Hall

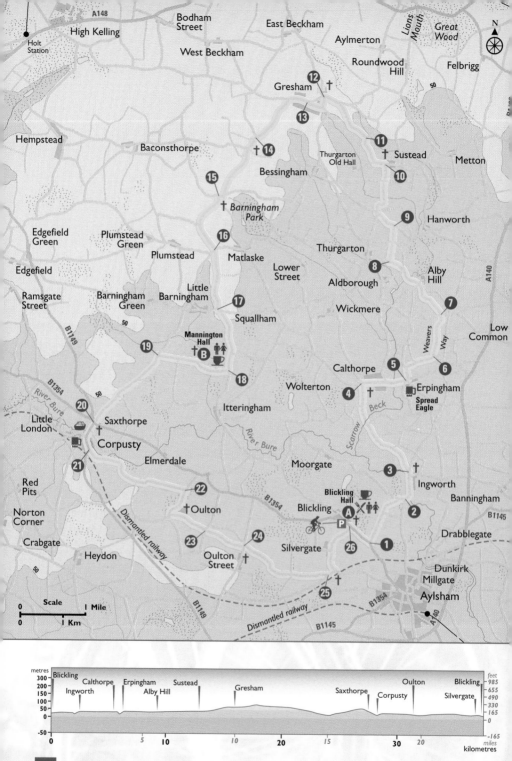

2 LHF and cross River Bure. Continue SO, SP Cromer, past St Lawrence's church.

3 LHF into Priory Lane. Continue through Scarrow Beck (ford) and SO uphill.

4 TR at staggered XR, SP Erpingham. Pass village church and continue SO, SP Erpingham. Cross Scarrow Beck again and arrive at Spread Eagle pub in Erpingham.

5 TL, SP Alby. Almost immediately TL in direction of Alby. Then, RHF, SP Thwaite Common.

6 LHF, following Weavers Way.

7 SO at staggered XR, SP Thurgarton (9.5km/6 miles). Continue along this road, passing village school on RHS and Chapel Lane on LHS.

8 TR into Harmers Lane. Continue to XR and SO, SP Sustead.

9 TL at TJ. Continue to XR where TR, SP Sustead.

10 TL at TJ, SP Gresham. Pass St Peter and St Paul's Church on RHS. As lane bends, take RHF. Continue and TL towards West Beckham.

10 TL at TJ, SP West Beckham.

12 TL at XR into Chequers Road, SP Bessingham (TR at XR to see All Saints, a fine Saxon church). Continue and TR at TJ, SP Bodham.

13 TL at TJ into Holt Road, SP Bodham (16km/10 miles). Continue SO then TL, SP North Barningham.

14 TL at TJ, SP Matlaske. Continue SO then RHF, SP Matlaske.

15 LHF, SP Matlaske. Continue SO (views of Barningham Hall and church on LHS), and follow SP Plumstead.

16 SO at XR, SP Wolterton. Continue SO, past farm track on LHS.

17 SO at XR, SP Itteringham. Continue SO, past lane on RHS, following SP Itteringham.

18 TR, SP Little Barningham. Continue SO, past private entrance to Mannington Hall on RHS (24km/15 miles). Then LHF, past public entrance to Mannington Hall.

19 TL at TJ, SP Norwich.

20 SO at XR onto B1149, SP Norwich. Almost immediately take RHF (staying on B1149) across River Bure. Then take LHF, SP Cawston.

21 TL into Irmingland Road, SP Oulton.

22 RHF, SP Oulton. Continue to XR where TL, SP Oulton Street (32km/20 miles), and continue SO, passing St Peter and St Paul's Church.

23 So at XR, SP Oulton Street.

24 SO at staggered XR, SP Aylsham. Beside this junction is a memorial to the airmen of the British, Commonwealth and American forces who lost their lives whilst stationed at RAF Oulton between 1940 and 1945.

25 LHF, towards Silvergate. Then TL at TJ, towards Silvergate. Continue SO, through Silvergate.

26 TL at TJ onto B1354. Pass Blicking Hall on RHS. Take LHF, SP Saxthorpe, and then TR into Blickling Hall car park to finish the ride.

37.5km (23.5 miles)

COLCHESTER AND DEDHAM

Route information

Distance   41.5km (26 miles)

Grade   Moderate

Terrain   Generally quiet roads.

Time to allow   3–6 hours.

Getting there by car   Colchester is 22.5km (14 miles) south east of Subury, off the A12 and A120. There is plenty of parking in the town, including a car park at Colchester North Station, the start of the route.

Getting there by train   There is a frequent service to Colchester North Station. See page 13 for travel information.

The route starts from Colchester in north east Essex and heads south east to Wivenhoe, then north to Dedham on the Essex/Sussex border, before heading back to Colchester. The National Cycle Network (NCR 1) is followed for much of the way.

Route description

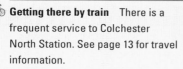

Join cycle path on RHS of Colchester North Station exit and cross bridge over A134. Circle left to pass under bridge and join cycle path alongside A134.

1   Take second exit at roundabout (use cycle lane). Pass Norfolk pub on RHS. Take first exit at roundabout, join cycle path and continue past fire station on RHS, DIY store on LHS.

2   SO across Mason Road and TR to join NCR 1. Cross Caudray Avenue (use crossing). TR and TL , past bowling alley, across cricket field and over footbridge. TL and follow path nearest river to East Street.

3   Cross East Street (use crossing) and TL to follow East Street as it bears right before river and continues between buildings to allotments, under railway line to river path. Continue, passing Millennium mile post (MMP) on RHS.

4   Staying on NCR 1, TR and TL into Spurgeon Street and continue to Back Lane.

5   TL and cross bridge by Hythe Station. TR into Hawkins Road.

6   Arrive roundabout, cross Hawkins Road and join cycle path (NCR 1) along Colrie Causeway.

7   TL (use crossing) across Colrie Causeway and join Wivenhoe Trail (NCR 1). Continue SO, past MMP on LHS and across Wivenhoe Station car park.

8   Take second exit at roundabout into West Street, passing Station Pub on LHS. TR at TJ into High Street, continue around Anchor Hill and TL at TJ into The Quay.   *8km (5 miles)*

9   TL, by Rose and Crown pub, into Rose Lane. Continue uphill and TR at TJ into East Street. Then SO at XR into Brook Street, which becomes Anglesea Road. Follow Anglesea Road right up hill and cross railway bridge.

10   TL into Queens Road, then TR into Valley Road. TR into The Dale, which becomes Claremont Road. TR at TJ into Baves Road, continue uphill and TR at TJ into Rectory Hill road. TL into Keelers Road, SP Elmstead.

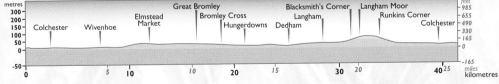

11 RHF into Tye Lane. Then TR at TJ uphill into Brightlingsea Road/B1027. TL, SP Elmstead. Pass Birds Farm holiday cottages on LHS.

12 TR at XR onto A133. Then TL into Branley Road.

13 Leave NCR 1 and TL at XR into Parsons Hill (B1029). Continue SO, across A12, past

Great Bromley village hall on LHS (16km/ 10 miles), then Mary Lane North on RHS.

14 TR into Bradley Hall Road, SP Little Bromley.

15 TL. Continue to TJ where TL towards Ardleigh. Pass Carrington's Farm, Liliers Lane and Hazels Farm on RHS.

16 TR into Briar Road and pass lane and orchards on RHS.

17 TR at XR into Water House Lane. Then TL at TJ towards Badley Hall and RHF, SP Lawford.

18 TL into Tithe Barn Lane. SO at XR, downhill. Then SO across railway bridge and uphill. SO at XR into East Lane and descend (24km/15 miles). TL at foot of descent and pass Castle House.

19 TR into Crown Street, downhill into Dedham and continue SO through village. Pass Parsons Field then Forge Street.

20 TL into Southfields and SO to join The Drift (a paved path) across playing fields.

21 TL at TJ into High Street. Pass assembly rooms on LHS. TR into Statford Road for climb and follow road crossing over A12.

22 TL at TJ uphill, rejoining NCR 1. TR, SP Langham (route now follows NCR 1) back to Colchester.

23 TL into Rectory Road. Descend and climb towards Langham.

24 RHF into School Road, passing MMP on RHS.

25 TL at XR into Moor Road, SP Colchester. Continue as Moor Road becomes Langham Lane. *32km (20 miles)*

26 TL at TJ into Severalls Lane, SP Colchester. Continue SO, across A12 and business park.

27 Take second exit at roundabout, staying in Severalls Lane (ignore cycle path on RHS and New Canen Way on LHS).

28 TR into Brinkley Lane and join cycle path. SO at roundabout across Gavin Way. TL across Brinkely Lane (use crossing) into Chinook Road and continue to Sea King Road. TR into Sea King Road. TL and follow cycle path through underpass, across Highwoods Square and Tynedale Square. SO at XR across Eastwood Drive into Briarwood End. Then TL at TJ to join cycle path. SO at XR across Chanterelle Road.

29 TR at TJ, along cycle path (Ipswich Road/A1232). SO at XR across Friars Close.

30 TR into Broadlands Way (leaving cycle path). TR into Havening Close, join cycle path and follow path beneath two railway arches. TR at TJ into Service Road (parallel to Caudray Avenue). Pass Halfords on RHS.
40km (25 miles)

31 SO across Mason Road. Pass Albert pub. TR at roundabout into Station Road North. Take third exit at roundabout, SP Sudbury, then first exit at roundabout, SP Railway Station/Saturday Park and Ride. Continue SO into station car park and finish the ride.
41.5km (26 miles)

Food and drink

Lots of choice in Colchester, Wivenhoe and Dedham. There are several pubs passed along the way. Refreshments are available at Bridge Cottage.

Colchester Castle

A Colchester

The town sits on the River Colne and dates from the Iron Age. Colchester was the first Roman capital of Britain and there are many Roman remains including the **town walls**, built by the Romans between 65 and 80 AD. **Colchester Castle** was constructed by the Normans between 1076 and 1125 on the site of a ruined Roman temple. The castle houses the town's **museum** which describes over 2000 years of Colchester's history. Also guided tours to the foundations of the Roman temple beneath the castle. Open all year, Monday–Saturday 1000–1700, Sunday 1300–1700. Charge. Telephone (01206) 282931. There is much else to see in Colchester, including Bourne Mill, Colchester Zoo and many museums and galleries. Contact the Tourist Information Centre for more details (see page 13), or visit www.colchester.gov.uk

B Dedham

An unspoilt village on the River Stour, in the heart of Constable country. The 16th-century church was funded by the wool trade. Visit www.dedham-parishchurch.org.uk for more details. Dedham has many fine buildings, including the old grammar school attended by John Constable. By the river there is a craft centre, restaurant and boatyard where visitors can hire boats.

C Castle House, Dedham

Castle House was the home of Sir Alfred Munning for over 40 years. Visitors can see a collection of his paintings, his studio and walk around the gardens. Open May to July and September, Wednesday and Sunday 1400–1700; August, Wednesday, Thursday and weekends 1400–1700. Charge. Telephone (01206) 322127.

D Flatford Mill and Bridge Cottage

John Constable was born in East Bergholt, just north east of Dedham. Close by is Flatford Mill, painted by Constable. Today the mill houses an educational centre but just upstream is 16th-century Bridge Cottage which contains an exhibition on Constable. Walks, boat hire and tea garden. National Trust property. Open March, April and October, Wednesday–Sunday 1100–1730; May to September, daily 1000–1730; November to February, weekends 1100–1500. Admission free. Telephone (01206) 298260.

NORTH NORFOK – HOLT AND BLAKENEY

Route information

Distance 41.5km (26 miles)

Grade Moderate

Terrain Generally quiet lanes and two short climbs.

Time to allow 3–5 hours.

Getting there by car Holt is 16km (10 miles) west of Cromer on the A148. Most of the town's car parks are short stay. Use the long stay car park, well signposted adjacent to the A148.

Getting there by train The nearest mainline railway station is at Sheringham, approximately 8km (5 miles) north east of Holt. Opposite Sheringham Station, the North Norfolk Railway runs steam and vintage diesel trains between Sheringham and Holt. Telephone (01263) 820800 for general enquiries, (01263)825449 for the talking timetable, or visit www.nnrailway.co.uk

From Holt the route heads north through Cley next the Sea to Blakeney. From here the route turns south and passes the location of the Bale Oak (a large tree in 1632, removed in 1860 – the area has been replanted) and makes a circuit to Hunworth and back to Holt.

Places of interest along the route

Ⓐ Holt

A pleasant market town. The many Georgian buildings are a legacy of a fire in 1708 which destroyed much of the town. Thomas Gresham, founder of the London Royal Exchange, was born here in 1519 and his brother John founded the Gresham School. The town is full of interesting antique and curiosity shops.

Ⓑ Cley next the Sea

Cley was once a busy wool port. Just east of the village is a road to Cley beach and access to Blakeney Point, a nature reserve well-known for colonies of terns and seals. The National Trust has an information centre at the far end of the point. St Margaret's Church was planned as a great building when work started in the 14th century, but the Black Death meant that there were few skilled workers able to finish the job. The church was originally in the centre of the village but a fire in 1612 destroyed so much of the town that the survivors moved to the northern end of town. There is a good delicatessen and a smokehouse in the village.

Ⓒ Blakeney

A harbour village, once a busy port. The attractive church, St Nicholas, has several outstanding features, including a fine hammerbeam roof and 15th-century font. The main tower is open to the public. The smaller tower was used as a lighthouse to guide ships into Blakeney harbour. Boat trips are offered to Blakeney Point.

Ⓓ Langham Glass, near Langham

Housed in 18th-century flint barns, visitors can

Cley next the Sea

watch craftsmen at work using traditional methods of glass making (selected days only). Also stained glass, wood turning, shop, museum and restaurant. Telephone (01328) 830511 to confirm opening times, or visit www.langhamglass.co.uk

Food and drink

There is a hotel, café and convenience stores in Templemore. The route passes a shop at Golden Crossroads.

Route description

If starting from Holt Station, TL out of station towards town centre. Start route at direction 1 where TR, SP Kelling.

From long stay car park, TL into Station Road. TR (before war memorial) into White Lion Street and follow this road as it bears R and becomes Cromer Road. Continue SO (as road bears L), past Gresham School and Grove Lane on RHS.

1 TL, SP Kelling.

2 TL, SP Kelling, and continue along this road, SP Kelling. Take LHF, SP Lowes, and cross Salthouse Heath.

3 SO at XR, SP Cley.

4 TL at TJ, SP Cley. TR at TJ, SP Cley. Continue on this road, SP Cley, as it descends (CARE) and bends R.

5 TR into Old Womans Lane and descend to salt marshes (good views).

6 TL at TJ onto A149, SP Hunstanton (8km/5 miles). Continue along this road, past access to beach and Cley windmill on RHS.

7 RHF, SP Blakeney. Pass Cley church. SO at XR for short, steep climb towards Blakeney.

8 SO, past St Nicholas church on LHS. Arrive five-way junction. Take second TR into High Street and descend to TJ at quay.

9 TL at TJ. Pass Blakeney Hotel and village SP and follow road as it bends L, past post office on LHS. Continue to XR with A149.

10 SO at XR onto B1156, SP Langham.

11 SO at XR, SP Langham/B1156. TR at TJ, SP Walsingham. Pass village SP on RHS, pub on LHS.

12 To visit Langham Glass TR at XR. To visit Langham village shop, SO at XR.

To continue route, TL at XR, SP Field Dalling. Continue on this road, following SP Bale.
16.5km (10.5 miles)

13 LHF, SP Bale. Continue SO along this road.

14 SO at XR, SP Gunthorpe. Pass Bale Oaks on LHS.

15 SO at XR, SP Gunthorpe. Arrive staggered XR with A148 and SO, SP Gunthorpe.

16 LHF and follow road past church on LHS. Take LHF, SP Swanton Novers, then RHF, SP Swanton Novers. Pass village SP on LHS.

17 RHF, SP Swanton Novers. Cross line of disused railway and old signal box. SO at XR with B1354, SP Swanton Novers.

18 TL at TJ, SP Swanton Novers. TR at XR, SP Hindolveston.
24km (15 miles)

19 SO at XR. Pass Swanton village SP on LHS, then St Giles Road on RHS.

20 TR at TJ onto B1110, SP East Dereham.

21 TL at XR, SP Hindolveston. Pass tiny church of St George Hindolveston and village SP. Continue SO, SP Thorning, then SP Melton.

22 Continue SO, past village hall and lane on LHS, then Station Road on RHS. Road bends R to cross disused railway.

23 RHF into The Dyes. You will see old railway platform and carriage. Then take LHF. SO at XR formed by lane and bridleway.

24 TL at staggered XR, SP Briston. Continue SO and cross ford.

25 RHF (leaving Greymere Lane) and pass lanes on RHS (32km/20 miles). Continue SO past Green Man pub and lane on LHS. Follow SP Melton towards church on LHS.

26 TR at TJ, SP Hunworth. Pass shops on LHS. Take RHF at next two junctions, passing church then post office and village SP.

27 Arrive XR with B1354 and SO, SP Hunworth. SO at next XR, SP Hunworth, for descent to Hunworth village green.

28 SO, SP Holt. Pass Bluebell pub on LHS. Follow road as it bears R and then climbs.

29 TL at TJ onto B1149, SP Holt (40km/25 miles). SO at roundabout, SP Holt Town Centre.

30 TR into High Street, SP Town Centre. Continue SO, past Holt town SP on RHS.

To return to railway station, take LHF and follow road back to station.

To return to car park, take RHF (before war memorial) into Station Road. TR, SP Car Park, to finish the ride.
41.5km (26 miles)

ATTLEBOROUGH AND HINGHAM

Route information

Distance 42.5km (26.5 miles)

Grade Moderate

Terrain Generally quiet roads.

Time to allow 3–6 hours.

Getting there by car Attleborough is 22.5km (14 miles) south west of Norwich on the A11. Most of the town's car parks have goal post barriers to prevent the parking of commercial vehicles. A car with roof mounted bicycles can access Edenside Drive car park, the start of the route.

Getting there by train Attleborough railway station is close to the town centre (no car park) and there are frequent services from Norwich, Cambridge and Peterborough. See page 13 for travel information.

This route starts from Attleborough and follows quiet country lanes to make a pleasant clockwise circuit north of the town, passing through several villages.

Places of interest along the route

A **Attleborough**

There has been a settlement here since Saxon times. Attleborough was known for its cider production and its turkey fair, the largest in the country. The herds of turkeys were walked to the London markets, their feet dipped in tar to protect them on the journey. Today market day is Thursday. St Mary's Church, once the centre of a much larger building, was built in the 12th century and contains a large 15th-century rood screen and wall paintings dating from circa 1500.

B **Hingham**

A pretty village with splendid greens bordered by Georgian houses, linked by narrow streets. The large church contains a bust of Abraham Lincoln, a descendent of Samuel Lincoln, a local weaver who emigrated to the then American colonies in 1638. For more information, visit www.hingham.ttrs.co.uk

Food and drink

Plenty of choice in Attleborough. There is a post office and convenience store in Rockland All Saints and pubs and a store in Hingham.

White Hart, Rockland All Saints
Meals available.

The Buck, Morley St Botolph
Food served.

IN THIS PARISH FOR MANY GENERATIONS
LIVED THE LINCOLNS
ANCESTORS OF THE AMERICAN
ABRAHAM LINCOLN
TO HIM GREATEST OF THAT LINEAGE
MANY CITIZENS OF THE UNITED STATES
HAVE ERECTED THIS MEMORIAL
IN THE HOPE THAT FOR ALL AGES
BETWEEN THAT LAND AND
THIS LAND AND ALL LANDS
THERE SHALL BE
MALICE TOWARD NONE

Inside Hingham Church

Route description

To start from Attleborough railway station, TL from Norwich platform towards the town (TR from Cambridge/Peterborough platform). TL into New North Road. TL at TJ into Connaught Road and continue into High Street. RHF into London Road, passing The Cock pub on RHS.

From Edenside Drive car park, TL then TL again to join Connaught Road and continue into High Street, past post office and Sainsburys on RHS.

RHF into London Road, passing The Cock pub on RHS.

1 TR into West Carr Road and continue to junction with A11.

2 SO at staggered XR, across A11, SP Butterfly Gardens.

3 TL at TJ, SP Hargham. Then TR, SP Rockland All Saints.

4 SO across ford near Swangey Farm.

5 TR at TJ, SP Rocklands. Continue to XR where TL, SP Rocklands.

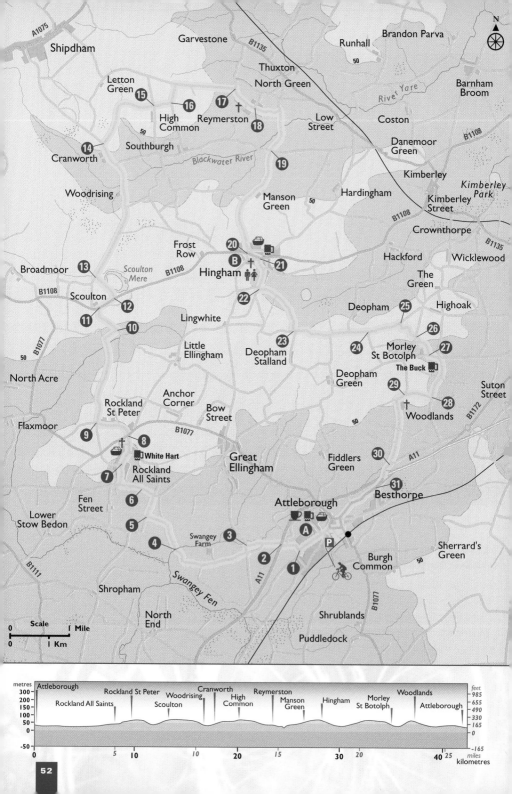

6 Continue SO towards All Saints Church and National School building, passing remains of church on LHS. Take RHF, SP Rockland All Saints, and continue into village.

7 TR at TJ (8km/5 miles). Continue through village, passing White Hart pub and post office/stores on LHS, then village hall and St Peter's Church on LHS.

8 SO at XR, SP Scoulton.

9 TR at XR, SP Scoulton.

10 TL at TJ, SP Scoulton.

11 TR at TJ onto B1108. Continue SO, passing Scoulton village SP on RHS.

12 TL into Mere Road, SP Village Hall.

13 TR at TJ, SP Cranworth (14.5km/9 miles). Continue along this road, through Woodrising and into Cranworth.

14 TR. Pass playing fields on LHS.

15 SO at XR.

16 TL at TJ, SP Garvestone. Then TR at TJ, SP Garvestone.

17 TR at TJ, SP Reymerston. Continue SO, past avenue of limes leading to St Peter's Church on RHS, then pass village hall.

18 SO to join Bateman's Lane (24km/15 miles). TR at TJ, SP Hingham, and follow lane uphill.

19 SO at XR, SP Hingham. Continue into village, following SP Hingham (ignore first LHF).

20 In Hingham, take second LHF across green past Lincoln's Coffee Shop. TL at TJ, SP Barford B1108. Follow B1108 down past St Andrew's Church on RHS, then White Hart on LHS.

21 TR (by Londis store, as B1108 bears left) into Hall Lane. SO at XR then LHF into Hall Manor Lane. Pass Low Road on RHS.

22 LHF, SP Deopham. Then SO, SP Deopham. *32km (20 miles)*

23 Continue SO, SP Wicklewood, and join Vicarage Road. Pass Deopham village SP. Then SO, SP Wicklewood.

24 SO, SP Wymondham.

25 TR into Mill Lane, SP Morley St Botolph, towards greenhouses.

26 SO at staggered XR, SP Spooner Row, and join New Road as it heads towards St Botolph's Church. Then LHF to pass church gates.

27 TL at TJ, SP Wymondham. Pass The Buck pub and TR at XR, SP Besthorpe/Chapel Lane. Then SO at XR into Golf Link Road.

28 TR into Wood Lane (before entrance to Wymonham College).

29 TL at TJ, SP Besthorpe. Then SO as road bends left, and pass St Peter's Church (38.5km/24 miles). Continue SO, SP Besthorpe/Attleborough.

30 TR at TJ and follow road over A11.

31 SO to join Mill Lane as it joins from left. Then SO into Surrogate Street. RHF into Connaught Road. Retrace route to railway station or TL into Edenside Drive to finish the ride at the car park. *42.5km (26.5 miles)*

CAMBRIDGE AND LINTON

Route information

Distance 46.5km (29 miles)

Grade Moderate

Terrain Designated cycle path out of and into Cambridge, and generally quiet roads elsewhere.

Time to allow 3–6 hours.

Getting there by car Cambridge is bordered by the M11, A11 and A14. Much of the city centre is closed to traffic and on-street parking is difficult. Park at the railway station, the start of the route.

Getting there by train There is a regular service to Cambridge Station. See page 13 for travel information.

From Cambridge the route heads south east through Fulbourn to Balsham. From here the route travels south to Linton and then turns north west, to follow a Roman road back to Cambridge.

Places of interest along the route

A Cambridge

The compact city sits on the River Cam in an area inhabited since the first century BC. The first college, Peterhouse, was founded in 1271 and the most recent, Robinson College, was founded in 1977. Visitors can walk through the college courts at most times – information on restrictions/charges is given on notice boards at the college gates. Public walking tours around the colleges are run from the Tourist Information Centre. There is much for the visitor to see in the city, including several fine churches, parks and gardens, museums and galleries and opportunities for boating on the river. Contact the Tourist Information Centre for more information or visit www.cambridge. gov.uk. Cambridge is a cyclist's city and there are lots places with bicycles to hire. However, bicycle theft is a problem – lock your bicycle securely when you leave it. A useful cycle route map of the city is available from the Tourist Information Centre.

B Fulbourn Windmill, near Fulbourn

A smock mill built in 1808 by a local landowner and farmer. The mill was worked until 1937 and today a local society is restoring the mill back to working order. Contact Cambridge Tourist Information Centre for more information or visit www.fulbourn.windmill.btinternet.co.uk

C Linton Zoo, Linton

A private zoo and wildlife breeding centre open since 1972. Lots of animals, birds and reptiles, in 6.5ha (16 acres) of landscaped gardens. Tearoom. Open all year, daily 1000–1800 or dusk if earlier. Charge. Telephone (01223) 891308.

Food and drink

Lots of choice in Cambridge. There are pubs along the route between Cambridge and Linton but none beyond Linton. Refreshments are also available at Linton Zoo.

Leave the station with covered pedestrian/ cycle bridge (PCB) at the northern end of the car park visible, SP blue bicycle. Join cycle path and TR to pass under PCB. TL to briefly join Devonshire Road then immediately TL and follow PCB as it crosses railway track. Descend to TJ with Rustat Road (ignore SP blue bicycle to Cambridge suburbs). TR into Rustat Road and continue SO, passing Darey Road and Fanshaw Road on LHS.

1 TL at TJ into Cherry Hinton Road (pedestrian/cycle path between here and direction 2). SO at roundabout across A1134, staying on Cherry Hinton Road.

2 SO at roundabout into Fulbourn Road, which becomes Cambridge Road. Continue and take second exit at roundabout, SP Fulbourn.

3 TL (in sight of windmill) and leave cycle path to join Hinton Road, SP Windmill School.

St John's College, Cambridge

Continue into Fulbourn, passing Bakers Arms pub.

4 RHF into Pierce Lane. Pass The Maples and Bird Farm Road on RHS. TR at TJ into High Street.

5 TR at TJ into Church Lane (Six Bells pub on RHS). Immediately TL into Manor Walk, SP Balsham. Road becomes Home End. Pass United Reform Church. *7km (4.5 miles)*

6 LHF, SP Balsham. Continue along this road to XR with A11, where SO and continue into Balsham.

7 SO, SP West Wratting, in High Street. Continue along High Street through Balsham. Pass The Bell pub on RHS. *15km (9.5 miles)*

8 RHF, SP West Wickham, and continue downhill.

9 TR at staggered XR, SP Bartlow, and climb. Continue to XR with A1307 where SO and continue into Bartlow.

10 SO at XR. Pass Post Office and Three Hills pub on LHS. TR at XR (22.5km/14 miles) and continue into Hadstock.

11 SO at crest of hill, past Moules Lane, for descent to TJ with B1052. *25.5km (16 miles)*

12 TR at TJ, SP Linton/B1052. Continue on this road, past Linton Zoo on LHS.

13 TL at TJ onto A1307, SP Cambridge. Then TR into High Street. Continue across bridge over River Granta.

14 TL into Symonds Lane then LHF into Back Lane and continue towards Little Abington.

15 TR towards Balsham. Then LHF onto bridleway, SP Leading to Roman Road.

16 TL at TJ onto Roman Road. *32km (20 miles)*

17 TL at TJ onto tarmac road and climb to cross A11. Continue SO ignoring road to Babraham. Then TL, leaving tarmac road, and rejoin Roman road.

18 TR onto tarmac byroad. Then TL at TJ to join Worts Causeway for fast downhill stretch.

19 TR at TJ into Lime Kiln Lane, SP Cherry Hinton, for steady climb. *40km (25 miles)*

20 TR at TJ into Queen Edith's Way (shared pedestrian/cycle path here). Continue and take first exit at roundabout into Cherry Hinton Road, SP City Centre. Then SO at roundabout, across A1134, into Cherry Hinton Road. Continue to Rustat Road.

21 TR into Rustat Road, leaving cycle path. Pass Fanshaw Road on LHS and SO to join cycle path.

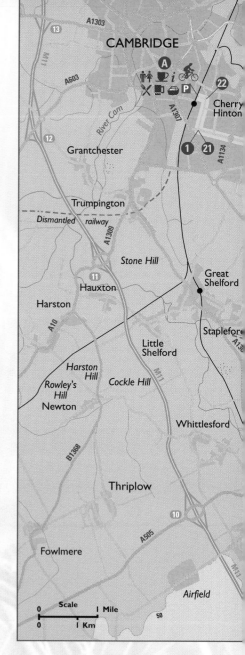

22 TL onto cycle path (leading only to PCB). Then TR at TJ into Devonshire Road and immediately TR underneath PCB and follow cycle path back to the station to finish the ride. *46.5km (29 miles)*

WOODBRIDGE AND THE DEBEN ESTUARY

Route information

 Distance   48km (30 miles)

Grade   Moderate

 Terrain   Quiet lanes through mostly flat countryside with just a few easy climbs. There is one section of off-road (tarmac surface), and a section of B road in the second part of the route.

Time to allow   4–6 hours.

 Getting there by car   Woodbridge is 12.5km (8 miles) east of Ipswich on the B1079. There are several car parks in the town, mostly pay and display.

Getting there by train   The route starts from Woodbridge Station which is on the Ipswich/Lowestoft line. See page 13 for travel information.

A circular route around the tidal estuary of the River Deben, taking in part of the Suffolk Coastal Cycle Route (SCR). From Woodbridge the route heads south past Newbourne Springs Nature Reserve to Felixstowe Ferry and crosses the river. The route now heads north back to Woodbridge. The area north of the river (a Designated Area of Natural Beauty) is known as the Suffolk Sandlings and is worth further exploration. Forest Enterprise has a cycle route here. Telephone (01394) 450164 for more information. Felixstowe Ferry operates Easter to October, daily 1000–1800. Charge.

Places of interest along the route

Ⓐ Woodbridge

An old Saxon town on the River Deben, once known for ship-building and sail-making. **Woodbridge Museum**, Market Hill, describes the history of the town and the surrounding area. Open Easter to October, Thursday–Tuesday 1000–1600, Sunday 1430–1630. Charge. Telephone (01394) 380502. The **Suffolk Horse Museum**, Market Hill, gives the history of the Suffolk Punch, the oldest breed of working heavy horse in the world, rescued from extinction in the 1960s. Open Easter to September, daily 1400–1700. Charge. Telephone (01394) 380643. Woodbridge has two restored 19th-century mills. **Buttrum's Mill** is a tower mill. Open May to September, Saturday, Sunday and Bank Holiday Mondays 1400–1800; other times by arrangement. Charge. Telephone (01473) 583352. **Woodbridge Tide Mill** is a rare example of its type. Open Easter and May to September, daily 1100–1700; April and October, open weekends only. Charge. Telephone (01473) 626618. For more information on Woodbridge visit www.debenweb.co.uk

B Waldringfield

Boat trips on the River Deben are available from here. May to October, daily, 1100, 1430 and 1830 (depending upon weather conditions). Charge. Telephone (01473) 736260 for more details.

C Newbourne Springs

A nature reserve situated by a stream in a wooded valley. A visitor centre is open daily, Easter to September 0900–1630; winter open at weekends only. Charge.

D Sutton Hoo, Sutton

Sutton Hoo is the burial ground of the Anglo-Saxon kings of East Anglia. There is an exhibition on the site and guided tours are led by the Sutton Hoo Society. Open Easter to October, Saturday, Sunday and Bank Holiday Mondays, guided tours at 1400 and 1500 (times subject to change). Charge. Telephone (01394) 411288.

Woodbridge

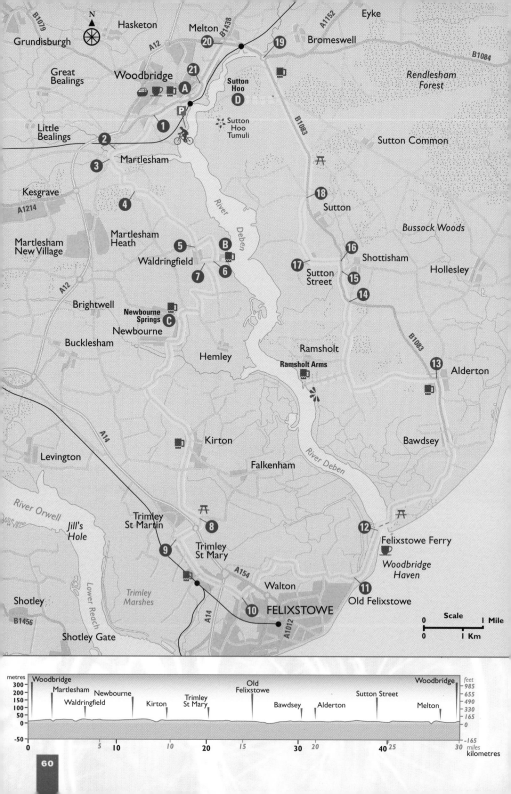

Route description

TL out of railway station.

1 TL by garage into Sandy Lane, no SP.

2 TL at TJ, SP SCR.

3 TL, SP Waldringfield/SCR for climb.

4 TL, SP Byroad/SCR.

5 TL at XR into Fishpond Road, no SP, and continue into Waldringfield.

6 To visit quay and pub, TL at TJ, no SP.

Otherwise, TR at TJ to continue route.

8km (5 miles)

7 TL into Mill Road, SP Newbourne/SCR. Continue along this road, through Newbourne (access to nature reserve) and Kirton, following SP Kirton/Felixstowe.

8 SO and cross A14 via bridge (do not use footbridge).

9 TL at roundabout, SP Trimley St Mary (21km/13 miles). Continue and again cross A14 via bridge.

10 TL into Gulpher Road, no SP. Continue along this road towards coast.

11 TL at TJ and continue to Felixstowe Ferry. *25.5km (16 miles)*

12 Catch the ferry across the river and follow road through Bawdsey to Alderton.

13 TL, SP Ramsholt (32km/20 miles). Stay on this road, passing access to Ramsholt Arms and dock soon after RH bend.

14 TL at TJ, SP Shottisham.

15 TL, SP B1083/Woodbridge. Continue and pass Sutton village SP.

16 Immediately after village SP, TL, SP Bridleway/Wood Hall Hotel.

17 Keep to RHS of hotel and TR, SP Byway.
39.5km (24.5 miles)

18 TL onto B1083. Pass picnic area on RHS and access to Sutton Hoo on LHS.

19 SO at roundabout, SP Ipswich.

20 TL at XR, SP Woodbridge.
46.5km (29 miles)

21 TL at XR, SP B1438/Ipswich, and finish the ride at the station. *48km (30 miles)*

Food and drink

Plenty of choice in Woodbridge. Several pubs are passed along the way. There is a café in Woodbridge and at Felixstowe Ferry.

Ramsholt Arms, Ramsholt
A good place to stop. Fine views of the river.

LAVENHAM AND WOOLPIT

Route information

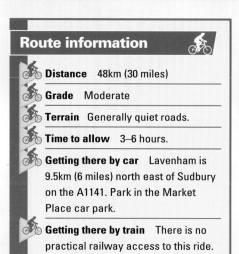

Distance   48km (30 miles)

Grade   Moderate

Terrain   Generally quiet roads.

Time to allow   3–6 hours.

Getting there by car   Lavenham is 9.5km (6 miles) north east of Sudbury on the A1141. Park in the Market Place car park.

Getting there by train   There is no practical railway access to this ride.

From Lavenham the route heads east to Kettlebaston and then turns north to Woolpit, with an optional extension to the Museum of East Anglian Life in Stowmarket (an extra 9.5km/6miles). The route continues through the villages of Beyton, Hessett and Great Green, and back to Lavenham.

Places of interest along the route

Ⓐ Lavenham
Lavenham is a former wool town, with many half-timbered buildings and a splendid church, **St Peter and St Paul**, rebuilt and financed by the town's wealthy clothiers between 1486 and 1525. Open daily, summer 0830–1730; winter closes 1530. The **Guildhall of Corpus Christi** is an early 16th-century timber framed building containing exhibitions on local history, the wool industry, farming and railways. Also walled garden. National Trust property. Open March and November, weekends 1100–1600; April, Thursday–Sunday 1100–1700; May to October, daily 1100–1700. Charge. Telephone (01787) 247646. **Little Hall** is a timber-framed wool merchant's house dating from the 14th century and restored in the 1920s and 1930s. Also garden. Open April to October, Wednesday, Thursday, Saturday and Sunday 1400–1730. Charge. For more information on Lavenham visit www.lavenham.co.uk

Ⓑ Museum of East Anglian Life, Stowmarket
The museum describes East Anglia's rural past. Also steam engines, farm implements and a working watermill and wind pump. Craft workshops and displays of Suffolk Punch horses at work. Tearoom and picnic area. Open April to October, Monday–Saturday 1000–1700, Sunday 1100–1700. Charge. Telephone (01449) 612229.

Ⓒ Woolpit
A pretty village featuring a pump at its centre, built as a memorial to Queen Victoria. The village's name is not derived from the local woollen industry but comes from the old English *wulf pytt*, or wolf pit, dug to trap the animals. During the Middle Ages the village was a place of pilgrimage for those with poor or failing eyesight who visited the healing waters of Our Lady's Well, believed to be located in field north of St Mary's. The church is constructed from flint and stone, parts of which date back to the 11th century. The landmark steeple was rebuilt in 1853 and is 42.5m (140 feet) high. **Woolpit Bygones Museum** depicts Suffolk village life through displays and photographs. Open April to September, weekends and Bank Holidays 1430–1700. Charge. Visit www.woolpit.org for more information.

Route description

Start in Lavenham's Market Place, with Guildhall on LHS. TL into Lady Street and head downhill. TR at TJ into Water Street. LHF into Lower Road, SP Local Traffic, and continue SO downhill.

1 TR at XR, SP Preston. Follow lane as it descends, crosses River Brett and climbs.

2 RHF, SP Preston/Byways South Suffolk Route 1A. Continue SO past Preston Priory barn complex.

3 RHF, SP Hitcham. Pass Six Bells pub and access to College Farm/St Mary's Church.

4 TL, SP Monks Eleigh. Continue SO, SP Kettlebaston. Cross River Brett and continue uphill into Kettlebaston. ***9km (5.5 miles)***

5 Continue SO through village for fast descent (CARE) to junction where TL into Bury Road and follow road as it bends and climbs.

6 TR and descend Dale Lane, SP Buxhall. Continue SO, following SP Buxhall, eventually climbing.

7 For main route, TL at TJ, SP Rattlesden and continue to direction 8.

To visit museum of East Anglian Life continue SO towards Buxhall (follow road as it bears right). Continue along this road, past Kiln Lane and Valley Lane on RHS, following SP Great Finborough.

a TL at TJ, SP Onehouse. Continue SO towards Onehouse. Pass tearooms on LHS.

b TR at TJ, SP Stowmarket. Continue SO. Pass Hill Farm and descend past tearooms and pub.

c TL at TJ, SP Stowmarket. Continue SO following SP Stowmarket/ Museum. TR into Illife Way towards Asda Supermarket to second car park entrance on LHS. TL here to Asda, shop and museum. After visit, recross car park and TR into Illife Way. TL at TJ and pass Childer Road and Recreational Road. TR, SP Openhouse/Leisure Centre. Continue SO (past Gainsborough Road and Chilton Way) and descend Union Road.

d TR at TJ, SP Harleston. SO past Harleston village SP. RHF, past Onehouse village SP.

e TL, SP Shelland Green. Continue SO past Shelland village SP and church.

f RHF, SP Woolpit. Then LHF, SP Woolpit.

g TL, SP Rattlesden. RHF, SP Bury St Edmunds, and rejoin main route. Continue to direction 11.

8 SO, SP Rattlesden (16km/10 miles) past Top Road on LHS. Descend (CARE) to junction in Rattlesden.

9 TR at TJ into Lower Street, SP Buxhall. SO past footpath, then pub and church.

10 TL, SP Woolpit, for steep climb.

11 LHF, SP Woolpit, and continue SO, following SP Woolpit into village.

12 LHF into Rags Lane. Continue to TJ, ignoring all estate roads on RHS. TL at TJ then TR at TJ into Drinkstone Road (two mills visible on RHS).

13 RHF, SP Drinkstone. Pass windmills. SO at XR, SP To Tostock, and continue uphill.

14 SO at XR, SP Hessett. Then RHF, SP Beyton (24km/15 miles). Continue SO into Beyton.

15 TL at TJ. Pass village SP on LHS. TL at XR, SP Hessett. Continue SO through village.

16 SO at XR, SP Hessett. Continue SO into Hessett, following SP Felshan. Pass church on LHS, pub on RHS. TR into Heath Road, SP Rougham.

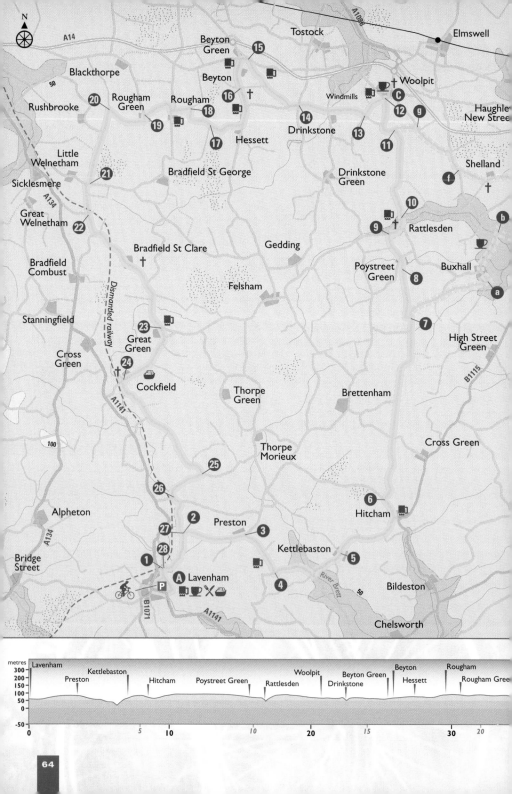

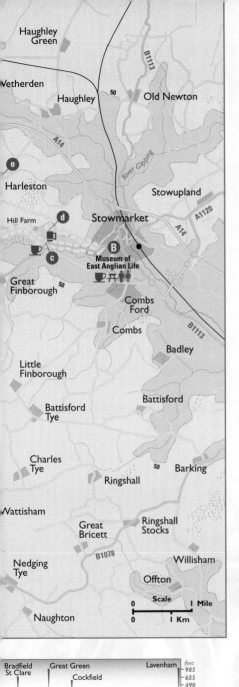

17 TR at TJ, SP Rougham.

18 TL at TJ, SP Rougham. Past Bennet Arms pub. TR at TJ into Moat Road, SP Bury St Edmunds.

19 TL at TJ, SP Rushbrooke. Continue to XR, where SO.

20 TL at TJ, SP Welnetham (32km/20 miles). Then SO, SP Welnetham.

21 TR at TJ, SP Welnetham. Then TL, SP St Clare.

22 SO at XR, SP Bradfield/St Clare. Continue SO, passing entrance to church. Then SO, SP Cockfield Green, and pass lane on LHS.

23 RHF, SP Cockfield. TR at TJ into Chapel Road, SP Cockfield village. Pass store, post office and access to church.

40km (25 miles)

24 TL, SP Bultons Green. Continue SO, past access to Earls Hall, and through Bultons Green.

25 TR at TJ, no SP.

26 TL at TJ, SP Preston. Then RHF, passing Rookwood Lane on LHS.

27 TR at TJ, SP Lavenham/Byways South Suffolk Route 1A. Continue into Lavenham.

28 TL at XR into Laver Road, SP Local Traffic. Continue along Laver Road. TR into Prentice Road and climb to Market Place to finish the route. *48km (30 miles)*

Food and drink

Lots of choice in Lavenham. The route passes several pubs. There are two tea-rooms on the optional section of the route.

MILDENHALL AND ELY

Route information

 Distance   48km (30 miles)

 Grade   Moderate

 Terrain   Generally quiet, flat roads.

 Time to allow   3–6 hours.

 Getting there by car   Mildenhall is 12.5km (8 miles) north east of Newmarket on the A1101. Park in the Recreational Way car park (off Kings Street, by the swimming pool).

 Getting there by train   There is no railway station at Mildenhall but Ely Station is close to the route. Leave the station, TR into Bridge Road (A142) and continue along this road (or shared use path) to direction 14.

This route takes you across the Fens. Starting from Mildenhall, the route heads north west out of Suffolk and into Cambridgeshire to the city of Ely. From here the route turns south east and returns to Mildenhall via the villages of Soham and Isleham.

Places of interest along the route

A Mildenhall

A town on the River Lark, dominated by the nearby RAF station occupied by the US Air Force. The annual Air Fete is the largest outside of the USA. Mildenhall also attracts hundreds of cyclists to its annual cycle rally. **St Mary's**
Church retains many features from the 12th and 13th centuries and has beautiful carved ceiling beams. The church tower is distinctive and can be seen on the approach to the town. The Tourist Information Centre (seasonal, in St Mary's Church) can supply details of a town trail, describing the town's history and interesting buildings. At the centre of Mildenhall is the Market Square, with a 15th-century market cross and pump. The **Mildenhall and District Museum**, King Street, describes the local history, including the story of the Mildenhall Treasure, a hoard of Roman silver found in 1942 and now in the British Museum. Open March to Christmas, Wednesday, Thursday, Saturday and Sunday 1430–1630, Friday 1100–1630. Admission free. Telephone (01638) 716970.

B Prickwillow Drainage Engine Museum, Prickwillow

The museum contains engines and artefacts associated with the drainage of the Fens. Also large photographic display. Tearoom. Open May to September, daily 1100–1700; March, April, October and November, weekends and Bank Holidays 1100–1600. Charge. Telephone (01353) 688360.

C Ely

Ely is in the centre of the Fens, on the River Great Ouse. The city is dominated by the **cathedral**, known as the Ship of the Fens. The cathedral was originally founded by Ethedreda in 673 and much of the present building dates from the 12th century. Open summer, daily 0700–1900; winter, Monday–Saturday 0730–1800, Sunday 0730–1700. Charge. The **Stained Glass Museum** is a unique collection of stained glass dating from medieval times, with over 100 pieces of glass displayed. Open summer, Monday–Friday 1030–1700, Saturday 1030–1730, Sunday 1200–1800; winter Monday–Friday 1100–1630, Saturday 1030–1700, Sunday 1200–1615. Charge. Telephone (01353) 660347. **Ely Museum** is housed in the old gaol and describes local history from the Ice Age to the modern day. Open daily, summer 1030–1730; winter 1030–1630. Telephone (01353) 666555. **Oliver Cromwell's House** contains exhibitions and period rooms, and the Tourist Information Centre. Open summer, daily 1000–1730; winter Monday–Saturday 1000–1700, Sunday 1100–1500. Charge for admission to museum. Telephone (01353) 662062. For more information on Ely, contact the Tourist Information Centre (see page 13) or visit www.ely.org.uk

D Downfields Windmill, Soham
The mill was originally built circa 1726 as a smock mill. After a storm, the mill was rebuilt as an eight-sided tower. It is still in operation today, and a range of flours are produced. Open Sunday and Bank Holidays 1100–1700. Charge. Telephone (01353) 720333; or visit www.soham.org.uk

Food and drink

There are opportunities for refreshment in Mildenhall and Ely. Several pubs are passed along the route, most of which serve food. There is a fish and chip shop in West Row and in Isleham, and refreshments are available at Prickwillow Drainage Engine Museum.

Route description

TL out of car park into Recreational Way. SO at XR into St Andrews Street. TR at TJ into High street and pass church on LHS.

1 LHF into New Street and TL at TJ into Queens Way. Continue along this road, passing RAF Mildenhall on RHS.

2 SO, SP West Row Fen.

3 LHF and continue into West Row. TL at TJ and follow lane past post office/chip shop.

4 RHF into Cooks Drove, SP Mildenhall Stadium. Continue SO, past stadium then Ranville Farm on LHS (8km/5 miles). SO between two bungalows at County Farm and cross drainage dyke.

5 TL at junction, following dyke on LHS. Continue SO and cross bridge over main drainage dyke.

6 TR at TJ towards pumping station, onto concrete road (road is below River Lark and runs parallel to embankment). Continue SO along this road (surface changes from concrete to shale and then to tarmac), passing World War II pillboxes, farm buildings, Engine Farm and Lark Engine Farmhouse on RHS. Then pass Flood Control Pumping Station and cycle through Lark Bank.

7 TL at TJ onto B1382 (away from level crossing). Continue along B1382, SP Ely, passing through Prickwillow (museum SP in village).

8 SO at level crossing to stay on B1382 through Queen Adelaide.

9 Continue SO on B1382 (20km/12.5 miles) and follow this road into Ely, arriving at High Flyer pub on RHS.

10 TL into Newham Street. Arrive XR at start of pedestrian zone and TR into Market Street. TL at TJ into Lynn Road.

11 TL at XR into High Street. SO at TJ into Forehill for descent. Then LHF toward Maltings (leisure complex) and river. Continue SO along Waterside Road to arrive at Waterside Antiques.

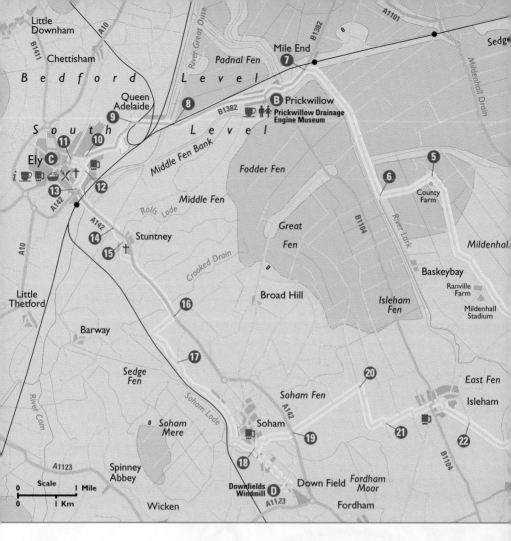

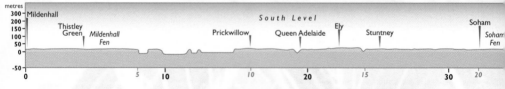

12 SO towards Quayside, following banks of Great River Ouse (beyond Maltings cyclists are required to dismount for short distance). Pass Cutter Inn and remount. Continue and RHF away from river into Annesdale Road. TL at TJ into Station Road and continue to roundabout.

13 First exit at roundabout, SP A142/ Newmarket/Railway Station (NB: there is a shared use path between here and direction 14). Continue along A142 as far as drainage dyke at Quanea Drove.

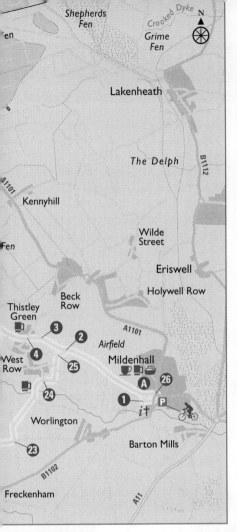

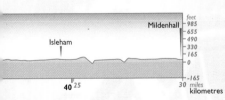

SP Newmarket, and continue along this road towards Soham.

16 TR off A142, SP Barway. TL (just before level crossing), SP Soham. Pass Logsmere Lane on LHS and Clarke Drove on RHS.

17 SO, past Julius Martin Lane on LHS and Spencer Drove on RHS. Continue SO into Clay Street and through market square.

18 To visit Downfields Windmill, TR at TJ into Sandstreet and continue SO into Fordham Road.

Otherwise, to continue route, TL at TJ into High Street, then TR into Brook Dame Lane, SP East Fen Common. Follow road as it bears left and becomes Paddock Street. Stay on Paddock Street and take RHF to cross East Fen Common.
33km (20.5 miles)

19 SO at TJ, across A142, SP Isleham.

20 TR at TJ, and continue on this road into Isleham.

21 TL into West Street. TR at TJ into Mill Street and continue towards St Andrew's Church. Take RHF, passing church on RHS, and join the Causeway. TR into Beck Road and then LHF, SP West Road. Pass Maltings Lane, SP Fordham.

22 SO, SP West Row. ***40km (25 miles)***

23 TL at TJ, cross old railway bridge and continue towards West Row. Then cross bridge over River Lark.

24 TR at TJ and bear left, SP Mildenhall. LHF into Potthall Road (ignoring Balsham Lane and track on RHS). Continue along Potthall Road.

25 TR at TJ into Chapel Lane. Then again, TR at TJ, SP Mildenhall. Pass airbase on LHS and continue into Mildenhall (road eventually becomes Queens Way).

26 SO at XR into Kingsway, then TR into King Street (by memorial). TR at XR into Recreational Way and finish the ride in the car park.
48km (30 miles)

14 At Quanea Drove, dismount, cross A142 to join path opposite, then TL into stopped road and head uphill towards Stuntney.
24km (15 miles)

15 LHF. Pass Lower Road and village SP on RHS, church on LHS. TR at TJ onto A142,

SAFFRON WALDEN AND THAXTED

Route information

Distance 49.5km (31 miles)

Grade Moderate

Terrain Generally quiet roads with some gentle undulations.

Time to allow 3–6 hours.

Getting there by car Saffron Walden is between Cambridge and Bishop's Stortford, just east of the M11. Park in the Swan Meadow car park (Bridge Street/B184). The town's other car parks are short stay only.

Getting there by train The nearest railway station is at Audley End, approximately 1.5km (1 mile) south west of Saffron Walden. See page 13 for travel information.

A circular route from Saffron Walden, once a major area for growing saffron crocus. The route heads south west through Thaxted to Great Bardfield, an attractive village with a stream and a fine bridge. From here the route turns north west, through the villages of Finchingfield to Helion Bumpstead and back to Saffron Walden.

Places of interest along the route

A Saffron Walden

Saffron Walden, named for the local cultivation of the saffron crocus between the 15th and 18th centuries, is an attractive town. Many of the fine old buildings survive, including the Church of St Mary the Virgin. A town trail is available from the Tourist Information Centre. The award-winning **Saffron Walden Museum**, Museum Street, describes the local history and also has displays on ancient Egypt and Greece. Open Monday–Saturday, March to October 1000–1700; November to February 1400–1630. Charge. Telephone (01799) 510333. **Bridge End Gardens** were first laid out circa 1794 by Atkinson Francis Gibson, whose son later added a Dutch garden, maze and a kitchen garden. Some areas of the gardens are open by appointment only, including the yew hedge maze. The public areas of the gardens are open all year, daily, dawn to dusk. Saffron Walden has a second maze, an ancient turf maze, on the common, the largest example of its type in the world. Close to Saffron Walden is **Audley End House and Gardens**. The house was originally built between 1603 and 1616 and is today furnished in the style of the 18th and 19th centuries. The grounds were designed by Capability Brown. Tearoom and picnic area. English Heritage property. Open April to September, Wednesday–Sunday and Bank Holiday Mondays 1100–1800; October Wednesday–Sunday 1000–1500. Charge. Telephone (01799) 522842. Visit www.uttlesford.gov.uk for more information on Saffron Walden.

B Thaxted

A historical town with timber framed buildings. The town's earlier prosperity is reflected in the huge 14th-century **church** and 15th-century **guildhall**. Church open all year, daily 0900–1800. Guildhall open Easter to September, Sunday and Bank Holidays 1430–1700. A town trail is available from the Tourist Information Centre. **John Webb's Windmill** was built in

1804 on the site of an earlier windmill. It has been restored and contains a museum. Open May to September, weekends, Bank Holidays and some weekday afternoons 1400–1800. Charge. Annual festivals of music and Morris dancing are held in the town. For more information, visit www.thaxted.co.uk

Food and drink

Plenty of choice in Saffron Walden and Thaxted. The route passes several pubs and village stores. Refreshments are also available at Audley End House.

Route description

To start from Audley End Station, follow SP Exit and TR at mini roundabout. Descend and TL at TJ onto B1383, SP Cambridge. TR, SP Audley End and continue to XR. SO at XR. Continue and TR at TJ into Audley End Road, SP Saffron Walden. Continue as Audley End Road becomes London Road (passing Audley End House and Gardens). SO at mini roundabout then second exit at next mini roundabout into Borough Lane. TR at XR into Debden Road and continue to direction 2.

From Swan Meadow car park in Saffron Walden, follow SP Exit and TR onto B184. SO at XR (traffic lights) into Hight Street. Climb past memorial, join Audley Road and take first exit at mini roundabout into Debden Road.

1 SO at XR. Then SO at mini roundabout in Landscape View, which becomes Debden Road.

2 SO at staggered XR, SP Debden.

3 RHF past SP Debden village. Continue through village, passing Plough pub on RHS.

4 SO at XR, SP Thaxted. *9km (5.5 miles)*

5 Arrive TJ facing Swan Hotel. TR into Watling Street and descend, passing Guildhall on RHS.

6 SO at TJ onto B184, towards Great Dunmow. Pass fish and chip restaurant and Star pub on RHS, then Rose and Crown pub on LHS. Take LHF, SP The Bardfields (opposite SP Thaxted village).

7 RHF, SP Great and Little Bardfield.

8 RHF, SP Great Bardfield. Then again RHF, SP Great Bardfield (18.5km/11.5 miles) and continue towards village.

9 TL at TJ, SP Finchingfield. Then RHF, SP Braintree, for descent past village stores on LHS.

10 LHF, SP Waltham Cross.

11 LHF, SP Finchingfield.

12 LHF, SP Finchingfield.

Saffron Walden

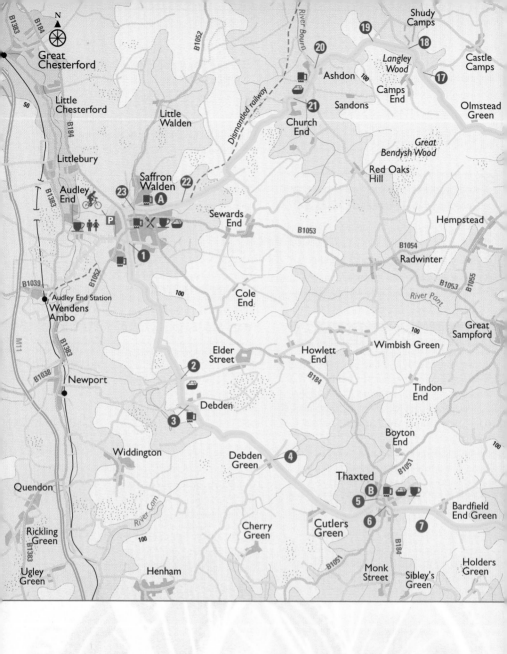

N

Great Chesterford

Little Chesterford

Little Walden

Littlebury

Audley End

Saffron Walden

Sewards End

Cole End

Audley End Station

Wendens Ambo

Newport

Elder Street

Debden

Widdington

Debden Green

Quendon

Rickling Green

Ugley Green

Henham

Cherry Green

Cutlers Green

Thaxted

Monk Street

Sibley's Green

Shudy Camps

Langley Wood

Castle Camps

Ashdon

Camps End

Olmstead Green

Sandons

Church End

Great Bendysh Wood

Red Oaks Hill

Hempstead

Radwinter

River Pant

Wimbish Green

Howlett End

Great Sampford

Tindon End

Boyton End

Bardfield End Green

Holders Green

B184 · B1383 · M11 · B1038 · B1039 · B1052 · B1053 · B1054 · B1055 · B1051

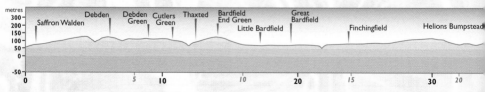

metres										
300	Saffron Walden	Debden	Debden Green	Cutlers Green	Thaxted	Bardfield End Green	Great Bardfield	Finchingfield	Helions Bumpstead	
200						Little Bardfield				

0   5   10   10   20   15   30   20

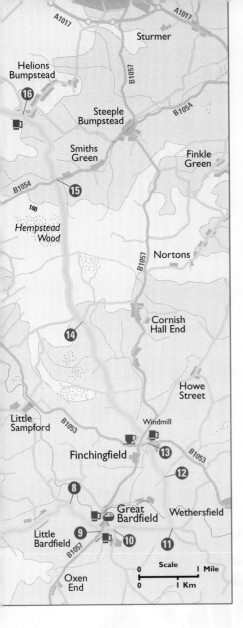

13 TL at TJ (24km/15 miles), and descend into Finchingfield. Take RHF, SP Steeple Bumbstead, and pass old windmill on RHS. TL, SP Helions Bumpstead/Spains Hall, and continue SO.

14 LHF, SP Great Sampford. Then continue SO, SP The Bumpsteads.

15 SO at staggered XR, SP Helions Bumpstead (32km/20 miles).

16 Arrive XR opposite SP Helions Bumpstead village and TL, SP Olmstead Green.

17 LHF, SP Bartlow, and continue SO, SP Bartlow.

18 LHF, SP Ashdon.

19 TL at TJ, SP Ashdon (41km/25.5 miles). Take CARE on fast descent with tight bends.

20 TL at TJ, SP Saffron Walden. Descend through Ashdon, passing war memorial and village SP on LHS. Then SO, SP Saffron Walden. Pass Rose and Crown pub and village stores.

21 Continue along this road, passing access to church and Fallowden Lane on LHS, farm access and Butler Lane on RHS, then Sewards Lane on LHS.

22 SO, past Ashdon Commercial Centre on RHS (48km/30 miles), and arrive outskirts of Saffron Walden.

23 SO at roundabout into Church Street, SP Long Stay Car Park. SO at XR.

To return to station TL at TJ into Bridge Street (B184). SO at XR (traffic lights) into High Street, which becomes Audely Road. Take second exit at mini roundabout into London Road, then SO at mini roundabout, then second exit at mini roundabout, SP Audley. Retrace route to station, passing Audley End House and Gardens.

Otherwise, TR at TJ into Bridge Street (B184). TL into New Pond Lane, SP Swan Meadow car park, and TR at roundabout into car park to complete the ride. **49.5km (31 miles)**

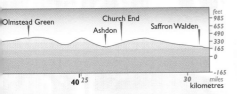

HALESWORTH AND SOUTHWOLD

Route information

Distance 54.5km (34 miles)

Grade Moderate

Terrain Mostly quiet lanes with a few stretches on B roads and a short section of busy A road.

Time to allow 5–6 hours.

Getting there by car Halesworth is 38.5km (24 miles) north east of Ipswich on the A144, just north west of the A12. Park by the railway station, the start of the route.

Getting there by train Halesworth Station is on the Ipswich/Lowestoft line. See page 13 for travel information.

From Halesworth the route heads south and east past Walberswick to Southwold on the coast, with an optional off-road section through Walberswick Nature Reserve (sandy tracks, suitable for mountain bikes only). Here the route turns north to Wrentham before turning west and back to Halesworth. The route takes in a short section of National Cycle Network (NCR 1).

Places of interest along the route

A Halesworth

Once known for its brewing industry, Halesworth is a small market town on the River Blyth with Elizabethan timber-framed houses in the market place. **Halesworth and District Museum**, Station Road, contains displays on local geology and archaeology. Also exhibits on local history and rural life. Open May to September, Tuesday–Thursday and Saturday, 1030–1230; Tuesday, Wednesday and Bank Holidays also 1400–1600. Admission free. Visit www.halesworth.blythweb.co.uk for more information.

B Holton Windmill, near Halesworth

An 18th-century post mill. The exterior has been fully restored. Open Spring and August Bank Holidays, otherwise by appointment only. Telephone (01986) 872367. The exterior can be viewed at all reasonable times.

C Southwold

A popular holiday resort. There is a lighthouse among the houses at the top of the cliffs. **Southwold Museum**, Victoria Street, describes local archaeology, geology, natural history and has displays on the Southwold Railway and the Battle of Sole Bay (against the Dutch in 1672). Open Easter to October, daily 1400–1600, August also open 1100–1230. Admission free. **Southwold Sailors' Reading Room** is a charitable institution founded in 1864. Visitors can see many maritime exhibits including pictures, model ships and figureheads. Open all year, daily 0900–1700. Admission by donation. **Southwold Lifeboat Museum**, Gun Hill, has a collection of RNLI related material and models. Open Spring Bank Holiday to September, daily 1430–1630. Admission free. Telephone to confirm opening times on (01502) 723600. The **Amber Museum**, Market Place, tells the history of amber, with carvings from around the world.

Open all year, Monday–Saturday 1000–1700; also Sundays July to September. Admission free. **Southwold Church** contains interesting decorative stonework, pulpit and screens. Open summer 0900–1800; winter 0900–1600. For more information on Southwold, visit www.southwold.blythweb.co.uk

Ⓓ Reydon Wood

Eighteen hectares (44.5 acres) of ancient woodland and green lane administered by Suffolk Wildlife Trust. Nature trail. Free access at all reasonable times. Visit www.wildlifetrust.org.uk for more information.

Route description

Leave the railway station and head downhill along Station Road. TL into Quay Street (CARE – busy road) and continue under railway line. Staying on B1123, take RHF, SP Blyford/Southwold (ignore LHF, SP NCN/Brampton/Beccles and SP Holton Village). Pass Holton Windmill on LHS.

1 TR (WITH CARE), SP Mells. Continue downhill, over two bridges, and take LHF, SP Wenhaston.

2 TL at TJ, SP Wenhaston/Blythburgh. Continue SO to green triangle/telephone box and take LHF.

3 TR at TJ (Compasses pub LHS), SP Back Road (4.5km/3 miles). Continue past Star Inn and road on RHS.

4 TR (second TR after Star Inn), SP Yoxford/Saxmundham. Climb up this single track road.

5 Cross A12 (CARE). TL at TJ towards Dunwich.

6 To follow off-road section, SO at junction into Walberswick Nature Reserve. Continue along track and rejoin route at direction 8 where

Southwold

continue on single track tarmac road, SP Footpath to Southwold (give way to pedestrians).

Otherwise, to continue route, TL onto B1125, SP Blythburgh/Walberswick.

7 To visit Tobys Walks (scenic walks and picnic area), TL at XR by water tower. Otherwise, to continue route, TR at XR (good views on LHS) and continue into Walberswick (11km/7 miles). Continue through village and past church. ***11km (7 miles)***

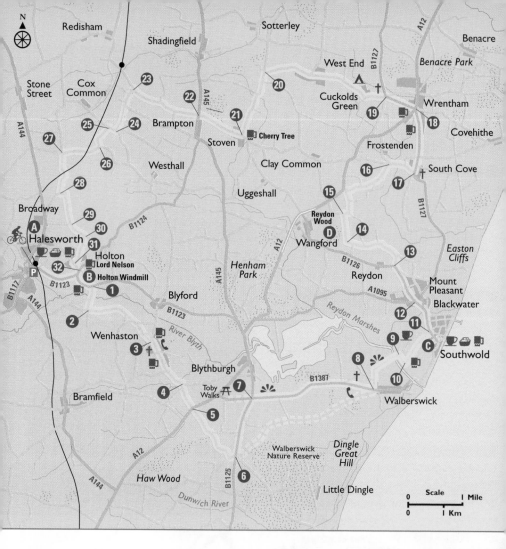

8 Shortly after church TL along single track road, SP Footpath to Southwold (give way to pedestrians). Dismount and cross bridge over River Blyth.

9 TR immediately after bridge and continue alongside river to Harbour Inn (this is a public footpath so please dismount and walk).

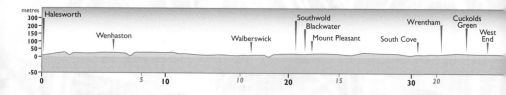

10 TL into Blackshore Road (by Harbour Inn).

11 To visit Southwold, TR at TJ (by Kings Head pub).

Otherwise, to continue route, TL at TJ.
19km (12 miles)

12 TR onto B1126, SP Reydon Church/Wangford. Continue past school buildings on LHS.

13 TR (just past school buildings) and take LHF, SP Wangford.

14 TR at TJ, SP Wangford. Pass Reydon Wood on LHS.   *27km (17 miles)*

15 TR at TJ, SP Frostenden. Continue approach to A12 and do a U-turn to follow lane into Frostenden.

16 RHF at XR, SP South Cove/Southwold.

17 TL at TJ onto B1127, SP Wrentham. Continue into Wrentham.

18 SO at XR into Chapel Road (CARE).

19 SO at XR, SP Sotterley/Shadingfield. Pass White House Farm campsite on RHS. Then take LHF, SP Stoven/Brampton.
34.5km (21.5 miles)

20 TL at TJ toward Stoven.

21 TR at TJ, SP Brampton 1.

22 SO at XR across A145 (CARE), SP Brampton Station. Continue towards station.

23 TL, SP Westhall/Halesworth.

24 TR at TJ, SP Bungay/St Lawrence.

25 TL, SP Spexhall (if you pass Methodist chapel or Racecourse pub, you have gone too far).

26 TR at TJ, SP Halesworth/Bungay. Pass under railway line.

27 TL at XR onto NCR 1 (no through road except for bicycles). Close level crossing gates behind you.

28 TL at TJ, SP NCR.

29 TL at TJ, SP NCR (49.5km/31 miles). Pass memorial to US servicemen on LHS.

30 TR (shortly after memorial), SP NCR/Holton.

31 TL at TJ, SP Holton.

32 TR at TJ, SP NCR 1. Take RHF onto B1123 and retrace route to Halesworth Station (CARE when TR into station on blind bend).
54.5km (34 miles)

Food and drink

Plenty of choice in Southwold and Halesworth. Most of the pubs passed along the route serve food.

 Lord Nelson, Holton
Food served lunchtimes and evenings. Outside seating.

Cherry Tree, Stoven
Meals available. Outside seating.

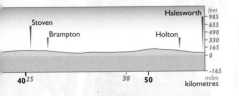

WISBECH AND THE FENS

Route information

Distance 60km (37.5 miles)

Grade Moderate

Terrain Quiet, flat but exposed roads. There is little shelter along this route, which will be strenuous if the wind strength is over 10mph.

Time to allow 4–6 hours.

Getting there by car Wisbech is 19km (12 miles) south west of King's Lynn on the A47 and A1101. There are several car parks in the town. The route starts from the Somers Road car park (off B198/South Brink), close to the town centre.

Getting there by train There is no practical railway access to this route.

This route makes a figure-of-eight circuit, exploring the silt fen to the south and the black fen to the north. From Wisbech the route heads south to Emneth in Norfolk and on to Upwell. From here the routes turns north and back into Cambridgeshire for the return to Wisbech. Once through Wisbech, the route makes a northward circuit to Tydd St Giles and back. Short sections of the National Cycle Network (NCR 1) are followed. As an alternative, each circuit could be ridden separately.

Places of interest along the route

A **Wisbech**

An ancient town and agricultural centre on the River Nene. The town grew up around its medieval port but the silting of the Wash means it is today no longer on the coast. Wisbech became a wealthy area during the 18th century, when successful landowners and merchants built elegant Georgian houses along the banks (brinks) of the River Nene. The **Octavia Hill Birthplace Museum**, South Brink Place, commemorates the life and work of Octavia Hill, founder of the National Trust. Open March to October, Wednesday, weekends and Bank Holiday Mondays 1400–1730. Charge. Telephone (01945) 476358. **Peckover House**, North Brink, was built in 1722 by a Quaker family. At the back of the house a walled garden contains summer houses and fruiting trees thought to be over 300 years old. National Trust property. Restaurant. House and garden open April to October, Wednesday, weekends and Bank Holiday Mondays, 1230–1730. Garden only open April to October Monday, Tuesday and Thursday 1230–1730. Charge. Telephone (01945) 583463. **Wisbech Castle and the Crescent** have been used as locations for television programmes and films. The castle was originally built in 1072 and in 1478 it was replaced by a Bishop's Palace. During the 17th century the present building was constructed as a private house by Joseph Medworth, who also built many of the surrounding Georgian villas in the Crescent. The **Wisbech and Fenland Museum**, Museum Square, is one of the earliest purpose built museums, dating from 1835. Displays describe the history of the surrounding Fens.

Open Tuesday–Saturday, April to September 1000–1700; October 1000–1600. Admission free. Telephone (01945) 583817. Real ales have been brewed by the Elgood family for over 200 years. **Elgoods Brewery** is open for guided tours and beer tasting. The gardens have been restored and include roses, herbs and a maze. Coffee shop. Tours available end April to September, Wednesday–Friday at 1430. Gardens open end April to September, Wednesday–Sunday and Bank Holiday Mondays 1300–1700. Charge. Telephone (01945) 583160. Wisbech Tourist Information Centre also houses the **Lillian Ream Photographic Gallery**. Lillian Ream was an early photographer and collected over 100,000 pictures of Wisbech and its inhabitants. Contact the Tourist Information Centre (see page 13) to confirm opening times. For further information on Wisbech visit www.wisbech.computer. co.uk or www.thisiswisbech. co.uk

B **St Mark's, Friday Bridge**
The village is known as the Pisa of the Fens for its church tower which leans at an alarming angle. The church was built in 1893 of yellow brick and the weight of the tower has caused it to sink.

Food and drink

There is plenty of choice in Wisbech. Several pubs are passed along the route and refreshments are available at Peckover House and Elgoods Brewery.

Route description

Leave car park via Alexandra Road exit (pedestrians/cyclists only) and TL into Alexandra Road. Continue to traffic lights. TR at traffic lights (five-way junction), SP Town Centre (Market Place). Pass monument on LHS

and TL into High Street, SP Market Place. TR into Market Place and SO, under iron arch into Church Terrace. Pass church and Dukes Head pub on LHS. TR at TJ then TL (immediately before Barclays Bank) into Stermyn Street. Follow one-way system into Orange Grove arrive pedestrian crossing of A110 (traffic lights). TL via crossing and join A110. TL into Norwich Road, SP Walsoken, then immediately TR into Elizabeth Terrace. Continue along Elizabeth Terrace to staggered XR.

1 SO at XR into Money Bank. TR into Quaker Lane (convenience store on RHS). Continue along this single-track road with XR with A47.

2 SO at XR into Meadow Gate Lane. Continue SO, past Oxburgh Hall on LHS.

3 TL at TJ onto A1101 (for short distance) and continue SO into Church Lane, SP Emneth. Pass village SP and church.

4 RHF, SP Outwell. Continue through village. Pass Gaultree pub on RHS. Take LHF. Pass Queens Head pub and take RHF.

5 TL into Fendyke Lane.

6 TR and follow metalled road.

7km (4.5 miles)

7 TL at TJ into Robb Lane. Take RHF and continue SO, SP Stowbridge.

8 RHF, SP Outwell. LHF into Angle Road. TR into Mullicourt Road.

9 TL at TJ onto A1122. TR across Well Creek (via Mullicourt Bridge) and follow creek towards Outwell, following SP Outwell.

10 TL at TJ then RHF. Pass church on RHS and TL (before bridge/A1101) into Low Side. Continue along this road as it bears away from creek and around houses.

11 TR at TJ and continue through Upwell. SO at XR into St Peters Road.

16km (10 miles)

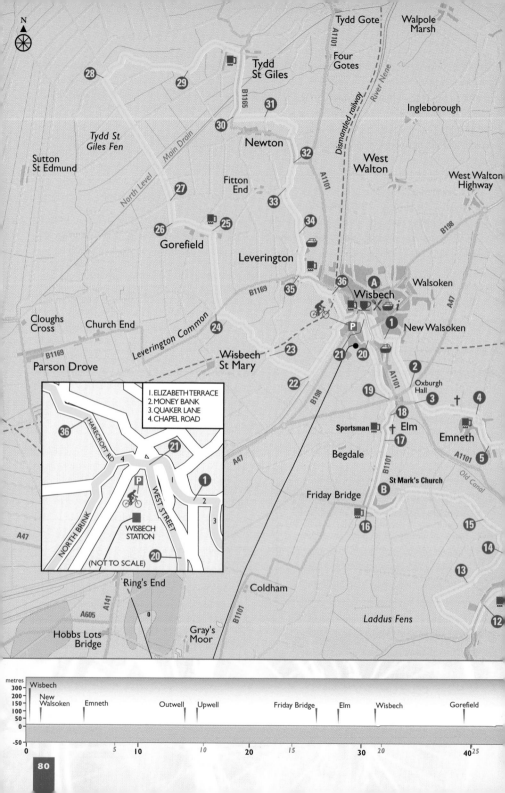

N

Tydd Gote
Walpole Marsh
Tydd St Giles
Four Gotes
River Nene
Ingleborough
Dismantled railway
B1165
Tydd St Giles Fen
Sutton St Edmund
North Level
Main Drain
Newton
West Walton
West Walton Highway
B198
A1101
Fitton End
Gorefield
Leverington
Walsoken
Wisbech
A
A47
B1169
Cloughs Cross
Church End
Leverington Common
New Walsoken
P
Parson Drove
B1169
Wisbech St Mary
Oxburgh Hall
Emneth
A1101
Old Canal
Sportsman
Elm
B1101
Begdale
St Mark's Church
B
Friday Bridge
A47
Ring's End
Coldham
B1101
Laddus Fens
A141
A605
Hobbs Lots Bridge
Gray's Moor

Inset:
1. ELIZABETH TERRACE
2. MONEY BANK
3. QUAKER LANE
4. CHAPEL ROAD

HARECROFT RD
NORTH BRINK
WEST STREET
P
WISBECH STATION
(NOT TO SCALE)
36
21
4
1
2
3
20

metres
300
200
150
100
50
0
-50

Wisbech
New Walsoken
Emneth
Outwell
Upwell
Friday Bridge
Elm
Wisbech
Gorefield

0   5   10   10   20   15   30   20   40 25

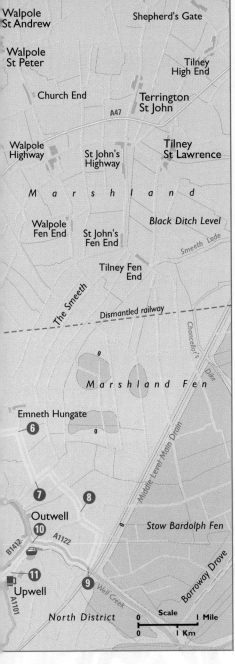

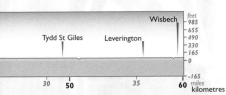

12 TR at XR. Cross Well Creek and TL. TR into Thurlands Drove.

13 SO, past two well-defined footpaths. Take RHF.

14 TL at TJ, SP Friday Bridge. LHF, SP Friday Bridge. Then RHF.

15 Pass Bramble Lane on RHS and continue along this road, eventually passing Molls Drove on LHS, then Kirkhams Lane on RHS (24km/15 miles), then The Stitch on RHS. Continue into Friday Bridge, following SP Wisbech.

16 RHF to pass between village SP and war memorial. Pass St Mark's Church on RHS. Continue along this road to Elm, past The Stitch on RHS, Back Road then Wales Bank on LHS.

17 Continue SO through village. Pass Sportsman pub on LHS and follow road as it bend past church, pub and lanes on LHS.

18 TL into Low Road and follow this road towards Wisbech. Pass Artful Dodger pub on LHS, through SP No Road Traffic to XR with A47.

19 SO at XR to join pedestrian/cycle link to Elm Low Road. SO at staggered XR into Elm Road as far as Flowerpot pub.

20 LHF into West Street. TL into King's Walk (just before Town Centre car park on LHS). TR at TJ into Alexander Road.

21 TL into Somers Road car park (the ride can be completed here).

To continue, leave car park via Alexandra Road exit. TL at XR into Alexander Road. Continue to traffic lights (five-way junction) and SO. Cross River Nene via Town Bridge and TL into North Brink (31.5km/19.5 miles). TL at TJ. Take LHF to follow North Brink alongside River Nene.

22 TR into Mile Tree Lane.

23 TR at TJ, then TL into Panswell Lane.

24 TR at TJ onto B1169, then TL into Wolf Lane, SP Gorefield. Continue to Gorefield.

25 TL at TJ into High Road. Continue SO through village and SO at XR, SP Parson Drove.

26 TR at TJ, SP Sutton St James.

40km (25 miles)

27 SO at XR into Cross Drove. Continue SO, crossing North Level Main Drain. SO at XR, SP Sutton St James. Continue SO, ignoring lane on LHS and pass former chapel.

28 RHF, SP Sutton St James. Ignore lane on LHS and continue SO into Park Road.

29 Pass Black Dyke on RHS. Lane zigzags. Continue into Tydd St Giles and take LHF into Hockland Road (49km/30.5 miles). Take RHF onto B1165, SP Wisbech/NCR 1. Pass village SP and church. Continue SO, re-crossing North Level Main Drain.

30 TL, SP NCR 1, leaving B1165.

31 SO, leaving NCR 1. Continue towards Newton. TR, following metalled road across dyke. Pass Goodens Lane and village hall. Follow Church Road as it becomes Rectory Road. TL at TJ onto B1165, SP Wisbech.

32 SO, SP Leverington, leaving B1165.

33 LHF, SP Leverington/NCR 1. Pass lane on LHS.

34 RHF, SP Leverington (56km/35 miles). Continue into village, past village SP and convenience store. TL at TJ, SP Wisbech/NCR 1.

35 LHF onto B1169, SP Wisbech/NCR 1. TR into Pickards Way (cycle access only), SP NCR 1.

36 TR at TJ into Harecroft Road, SP NCR 1. LHF into Chapel Road, SP NCR 1. TR into North Street, SP NCR 1. Cross River Nene via Town Bridge. Arrive traffic lights (five-way junction) and TR into South Brink. TL into Somers Road, SP car park, and finish the ride in the car park.

60km (37.5 miles)

Near Upwell

KING'S LYNN AND WEST NORFOLK

Route information

Distance   75.5km (47 miles)

Grade   Moderate

Terrain   No severe climbs, just a few gentle rises. However, the flat open landscape means that this route is best avoided when the winds are strong.

Time to allow   4–6 hours.

Getting there by car   King's Lynn is 62.5km (39 miles) west of Norwich on the A10, A47 and A149. There are long-stay car parks in Clough Lane and Boal Street.

Getting there by train   The route starts from King's Lynn Station. See page 13 for travel information.

This route takes you across the Fens, a vast area of marshland transformed during the 17th century by drainage canals. From King's Lynn the route heads south, following the River Great Ouse to the pleasant market town of Downham Market. Turning east, the route goes on to Oxborough before turning north back to King's Lynn. The route follows sections of the National Cycle Network (NCR 1) out of and into King's Lynn.

Route description

From Clough Lane car park TL into Blackfriars Street. Continue SO into New Conduit Street. TR at XR into High Street and continue to direction 2.

From Boal Street car park, TR at exit into Boal Street. TR at XR into Bridge Street. TR into Friars Walk, SP NCR 1. Pass roads of terraced houses on LHS. TR, SP NCR 1, and follow shared use path along eastern bank of Great River Ouse. Continue route at direction 3.

From the railway station, TL, joining NCR 1. TR at TJ. SO at XR, SP NCR 1, into Blackfriars Street (cycle lane here).

1   Pass Clough Lane and continue SO, following NCR 1 into New Conduit Street. TR at XR into High Street, SP NCR 1.

2   TL at TJ, SP NCR 1. Then TL into Church Street, SP NCR 1. SO at XR into Bridge Street, SP NCR 1. Pass Boal Street on RHS. TR into Friars Walk, SP NCR 1. Pass roads of terraced houses on LHS. TR, SP NCR 1, and follow shared path along eastern bank of Great River Ouse.

3   TL, descend flood bank and join St Valery Lane. TR at TJ, SP NCR 1, and join shared use path along Wisbech Road. TL, SP NCR 1. Cross Wisbech Road (via crossing). Follow SP NCR 1 and cross Saddlebow Road (via crossing). TR, SP NCR 1, and join road as it heads towards A47.

4   SO at roundabout, SP Wiggenshall St German/NCR 1. Pass Maple Road on RHS and continue to roundabout.

5   Take second exit at roundabout, SP Wiggenshall St German.

6   TR towards river.

7   Follow road L, past Fallow Pipe Road on RHS. Continue into Wiggenshall St German, past village SP on LHS and lanes on both sides.

8km (5 miles)

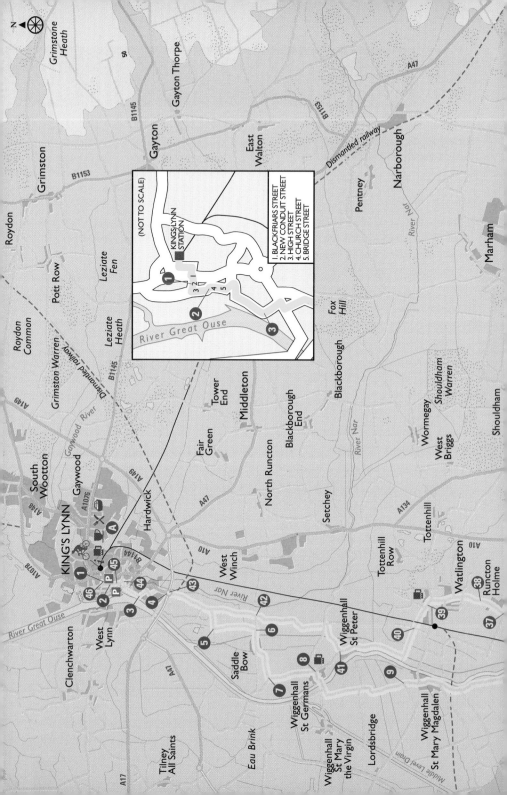

N

Grimstone
Heath

Gayton Thorpe

Gayton

East
Walton

A47

Narborough

River Nar

Marham

Dismantled railway

Pentney

Roydon

Grimston

B1153

Pott Row

Leziate
Fen

Leziate
Heath

B1145

Roydon
Common

Grimston Warren

Dismantled railway

Fox
Hill

Blackborough

Marham

Shouldham

(NOT TO SCALE)

KING'S LYNN
STATION

1. BLACKFRIARS STREET
2. NEW CONDUIT STREET
3. HIGH STREET
4. CHURCH STREET
5. BRIDGE STREET

River Great Ouse

Tower
End

Middleton

Blackborough
End

Wormegay

Shouldham
Warren

West
Briggs

Shouldham

A149

Gaywood River

South
Wootton

Gaywood

Hardwick

Fair
Green

North Runcton

Setchey

A134

Tottenhill

King's Lynn

A148

A47

A10

West
Winch

Tottenhill
Row

Tottenhill

Watlington

A10

Runcton
Holme

A1078

River Great Ouse

West
Lynn

B1144

River Nar

Wiggenhall
St Peter

A10

Clenchwarton

Saddle
Bow

Wiggenhall
St Germans

Lordsbridge

Wiggenhall
St Mary
Magdalen

Tilney
All Saints

A17

Eau Brink

Wiggenhall
St Mary
the Virgin

Middle Level Drain

A47

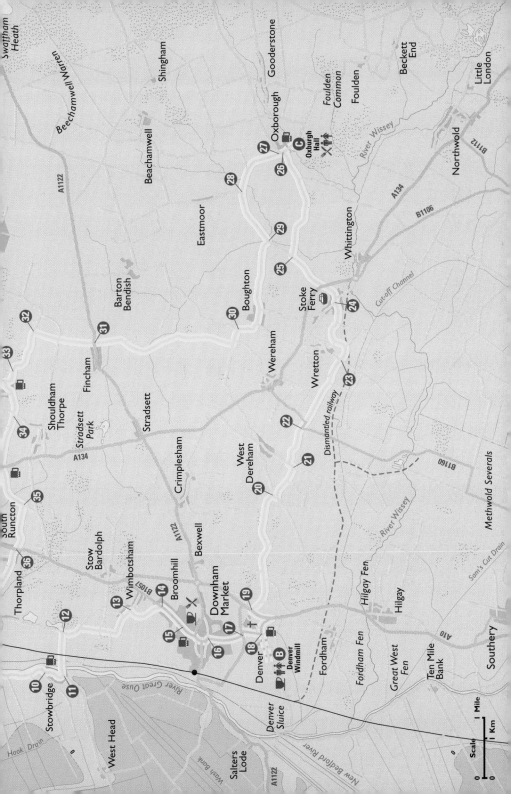

8 SO past Crown and Anchor pub and follow road as it bends R and crosses River Great Ouse. LHF, SP Wiggenshall St Magdalen/Fitton Road.

9 TL at TJ, SP Magdalen. Follow this road alongside River Great Ouse for approximately 4.5km (3 miles), past access to St Magdalen's Church, Mill Road and lane on RHS.

10 SO at XR. *16km (10 miles)*

11 TL at TJ, SP Runcton Holme. Continue SO, across River Great Ouse, drain and railway level crossing.

12 TR, SP Wimbotsham, at this and next junction.

13 TR, SP Downham Market, past village hall and Wimbotsham village SP on LHS.

14 TR at TJ onto B1507 (Llynn Road) towards Downham Market and continue to outskirts of town.

15 Continue SO, past post office, Cock Tavern pub and Clarkclose Road on RHS. SO at XR, SP Town Centre. Join one-way system and TR into Priory Lane, SP Town Centre. Continue to end of Priory Lane where TR at TJ into Bridge Street, SP Town Centre. TL at TJ into High Street, SP All Routes. Then TR at TJ (opposite Castle Hotel).

16 TR at XR into Church Road, SP Wisbech/A1122 (24km/15 miles). Follow SP Police Station to junction with A1112.

17 TL at TJ onto A1112, SP Denver. TR, SP Denver, past Denver village SP.

18 To visit Denver Windmill TR.

Otherwise, continue SO, ignoring lanes on both sides. Pass church on LHS and The Bull pub on RHS. TL at TJ onto A10, SP King's Lynn.

19 TR, SP Ryston Road. Take LHF and continue SO.

20 TR, SP Hilgay. Take LHF, SP West Dereham.

21 TL at TJ into Church Road. Pass West Dereham village SP on LHS. TR, SP Wretton. Pass village hall.

22 TL at TJ onto B1160. TR, SP Wretton. Continue, ignoring lane on LHS.
32km (20 miles)

23 SO at XR, SP Stoke Ferry. Pass Limehouse Drove and School Lane on RHS.

24 TR at TJ into High Street, SP Methwold. Continue to convenience store at next junction, where TL. Follow this road to end, dismount and walk short distance to XR with A134. SO at XR, SP Oxborough. Then TR, SP Oxborough.

25 SO, past Ferry Road on RHS and ornate gates of Oxburgh Hall. *40.5km (25 miles)*

26 Arrive complex junction. Take LHF. To visit village or Oxburgh Hall TR and follow SP.

To continue route, TL, SP Eastmoor.

27 LHF, SP Stoke Ferry. Follow lane across stream.

28 TL, SP Boughton.

29 TR at TJ into Chapel Lane, SP Barton

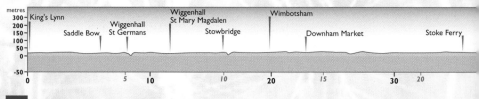

Bendish. Pass Boughton village SP, pond and lane on LHS.

30 TL, SP Wereham. Then TR, SP Fincham. Continue SO, ignoring lanes joining on either side (49km/30.5 miles), and head towards Fincham.

31 SO at staggered XR, SP Shoulderham. SO at XR. Pass Anglian Water Station.

32 TL at TJ, SP Shoulderham. Pass track to church.

33 LHF, SP Downham Market. Pass Shoulderham village SP on RHS and Kings Arms pub on LHS. Continue on this road.

34 SO past shell of former windmill (57km/35.5 miles) to XR with A134. SO at XR.

35 TR into Barnfield Lane, SP South Runcton. Continue to XR with A10.

36 SO at staggered XR with A10 into School Road, SP Runcton Holme. Pass College Lane on RHS.

37 TR at XR, SP Watlington.

38 SO, SP Magdalen. Then take LHF, SP Magdalen. Pass The Angel pub.
64km (40 miles)

39 TR, SP Germans. Continue SO across railway line and pass Polver Pumping Station.

40 SO at staggered XR, SP NCR 1.

41 SO, SP NCR 1.

42 Take third exit at roundabout, SP King's Lynn/NCR 1. Pass Maple Road on LHS.
72.5km (45 miles)

43 SO at roundabout into Saddlebow Road, SP South Lynn/NCR 1. Continue to crossing and TL, SP NCR 1/Town Centre, to join cycle path linking Saddlebow Road and Wisbech Road. Cross Wisbech Road via crossing. TR and follow cycle path, SP NCR 1. TL into St Valery Lane, SP NCR 1. TR, SP NCR 1, and follow shared use path along eastern bank of River Great Ouse.

44 TL at TJ, SP NCR 1. Pass roads of terraced houses on RHS. Continue SO through Friars Walk and TL into Bridge Street, SP NCR 1.

45 To return to Boal Street car park, TL at XR.

Otherwise, SO at XR into Church Road, SP NCR 1. TL at TJ, SP NCR 1. Then TR into High Street and TR at XR into New Conduit Street. TR into Blackfriars Street.

46 To return to Clough Lane car park, TR.

Otherwise, SO, SP NCR 1. Join cycle path alongside St Johns Terrace. TL into railway station to finish the ride. *75.5km (47 miles)*

Food and drink

Plenty of choice in King's Lynn. Several pubs are passed along the route and refreshments are available at Denver Windmill and Oxburgh Hall.

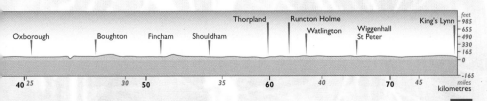

Places of interest along the route

A King's Lynn

The town was mentioned in the Domesday Book and rose to prominence during the Middle Ages, when it became the fourth largest town in England due its location on the River Great Ouse. Some of the fine buildings built by the wealthy merchants remain, including St George's Guildhall, dating from 1410 and the oldest guildhall in the country. Today it is part of the King's Lynn Art Centre. Other attractions include the Old Gaol House, the Custom House (now the Tourist Information Centre) and Purfleet Quay. Contact the Tourist Information Centre for more details (see page 13) or visit www.kingslynn.org

B Denver Windmill

A restored working windmill. The visitor centre describes the history of windmills and the people who lived and worked in them. Guided tours available. Also craft workshops, bakery and tearoom. Open April to October, Monday–Saturday 1000–1700, Sunday 1200–1700; November to March, Monday–Saturday 1000–1600, Sunday 1200–1600. Charge for guided tours. Telephone (01366) 384009; www.denvermill.co.uk

C Oxburgh Hall

A moated house built in 1482. Visitors can see the Tudor gatehouse, the 16th-century priest's hole. Also gardens and woodland walks. Shop and restaurant. National Trust property. House open March to October, Saturday–Wednesday 1300–1700; Bank holiday Mondays 1100–1700. Garden open March to October, Saturday–Wednesday 1200–1730. Charge. Telephone (01366) 328258; www.nationaltrust.org

Oxburgh Hall

THETFORD AND DISS

Route information

Distance 78km (48.5 miles)

Grade Moderate

Terrain Generally quiet minor roads with a few short stretches along busier A and B roads.

Time to allow 4–8 hours.

Getting there by car Thetford is 19km (12 miles) north of Bury St Edmunds on the A11. There are several car parks in the town.

Getting there by train The route starts from Thetford Station but can alternatively be started from Diss Station. See page 13 for travel information.

A route through south Norfolk. From Thetford the route heads north east and then south east to arrive in Diss. From here the route follows quiet lanes to East Harling from where it runs alongside the River Thet back to Thetford.

Route description

If starting from Diss Station, leave car park along Station Road as far as A134. TR at TJ onto A134 and, past railway bridge, join cycle path on RHS. Continue on cycle path, crossing A134, Skelton Road and Whytehead

Gardens. TR into Chapel Street. Then TR into Mere Street, dismount (pedestrian area) and continue to Market Place. TL at TJ into Market Hill and follow route from direction 23.

From Thetford Station, exit and TR into Canterbury Way. TR and follow single track road beneath railway line for gentle climb to TJ. TR at TJ into Munford Road (A134) and pass Station Lane on RHS.

1 TL into Croxton Road, SP Church of the Nazarene, and pass entrance to Breckland Leisure Centre. Continue SO along this road, beneath A11 and through Croxton.

2 SO, SP Munford, passing Croxton village SP on RHS.

3 TR at TJ, SP East Wretham

4 TL at TJ, SP East Wretham. *8km (5 miles)*

5 RHF, SP East Wretham. SO at XR, SP Illington, and continue to junction with A1075.

6 TR onto A1075, then TL, SP Illington. Cross humpback bridge and continue SP along this road, crossing Peddars Way and passing access to Illington. *14.5km (9 miles)*

7 TL at TJ, away from A11, and continue SO, past lane on RHS and across river.

8 TR to join Church Road (after crossing river).

9 TR, cross ford and continue SO.

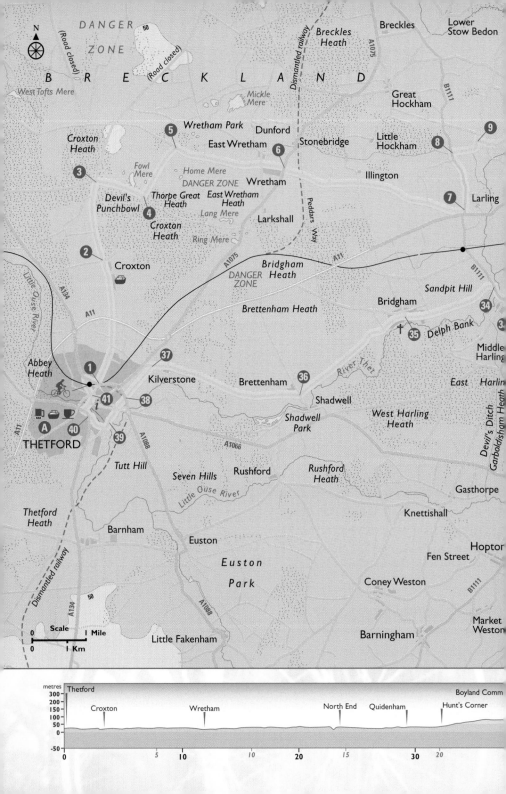

10 TR at TJ, passing front entrance of Watton Produce on RHS. Cross river again and continue SO at XR, SP Old Buckenham.

24km (15 miles)

11 SO at XR with A11 (CARE), SP Quidenham.

12 TR, SP Quidenham. SO at railway crossing and past Old Railway Tavern.

13 SO at XR, SP Quidenham. Ignore TR to St Mary's Church. Then take LHF, SP Quidenham, and continue through village.

14 TL, SP The Hospice.

15 TR, SP Banham. Take LHF then TL, SP New Buckenham.

16 TR at XR into Green Lane (32km/20 miles). Pass entrance to Banham Zoo.

17 TL, passing zoo on RHS. Take RHF, SP Winfarthing, then again RHF, SP Winfarthing.

18 TR at TJ onto B1077. TR into Dog Lane, SP Boyland Common.

19 TL into Common Lane, SP Shelfanger. Continue SO, ignoring roads on RHS and High London Lane on LHS. *40km (25 miles)*

20 SO at XR with B1077, into Rectory Lane. LHF into Heywood Road and follow road as it twists and crosses ford.

21 TR at TJ, SP Diss.

22 TR at TJ into Heywood Road, SP Diss. Continue SO, SP Town Centre (Heywood Road becomes Mount Street and descends to Diss market place.

23 If returning to Diss Station, TL at TJ and retrace route to station.

Otherwise, to continue route, TR at TJ, up Market Hill. Then TL at TJ into St Nicholas Street. SO at staggered XR with B1077, into Roydon Road. SO at next XR and continue along Roydon Road.

24 RHF into Brewers Green Lane. Continue SO, SP Bressingham.

25 TR at TJ into Snow Street.

48km (30 miles)

26 LHF, SP Bressingham. RHF, SP Bressingham. Then LHF into High Road, SP Bressingham. Continue through village (post office/village store on LHS).

27 To visit Bressingham Steam Museum and Gardens, TL at XR to TJ with A1066. TL along A1066 for approximately 300m.

Otherwise, to continue route, SO at XR, SP Fersfield.

28 RHF, SP Fersfield. Then LHF, SP Fersfield.

29 TR at TJ, SP Fersfield Airfield. Pass Fersfield village SP and church on RHS and TL into Bates Lane.

30 TL at TJ at The Common. Continue SO, passing entrance to Kenninghall Place Farm (55.5km/34.5 miles), Red Lion pub on LHS and St Mary's Church on RHS.

31 TL at XR, SP Garboldisham.

32 TR into Long Lane, then immediately TL,

SP Telegraph Hill (Kenninghall village SP on verge). Continue SO, past windmill on LHS, into East Harling.

33 TR at TJ onto B1111, SP Watton. Continue SO through village, following SP Watton/B1111.

34 TL, SP Bridgham. Continue into Bridgham. *64km (40 miles)*

35 SO, SP Brettingham. Continue along this road, passing St Mary's Church and minor road on LHS and crossing Peddars Way.

36 SO, SP Kilverstone. Continue past Langmere Boxes stables on RHS, entrance to St Andrew's on LHS and village memorial on RHS. Arrive Thetford Garden Centre on LHS and:

37 TL, SP Cycle Path, to Thetford Town Centre (74km/46 miles). Continue SO, past cycle path link to Kilverstone. Then SO at TJ as cycle path crosses Mallow Road, SP Town Centre.

38 Arrive TJ with A1088. SO into Toucan Lane (use crossing). Then SO at TJ into Castle Lane. Continue past Ford Place Retirement Home.

39 TL into Nunn's Bridge Road. Follow road across three single track bridges. TR into Mill Lane and follow river towards town centre.

40 TR at TJ onto A134. Follow road as it bends left. Then TR into Bridge Street, SP Car Park. Continue SO, crossing Town Bridge. SO at traffic lights into Whitehart Street. Pass Tourist

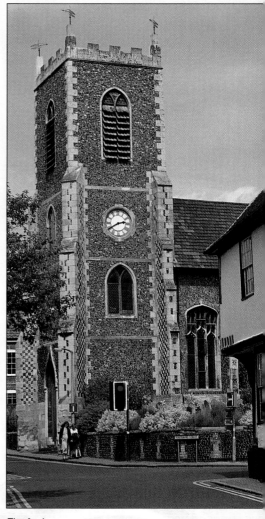

Thetford

Information Centre on RHS, reach stopped road and join cycle path to A1075.

41 SO at TJ with A1075 into Station Road (use crossing), SP Railway Station. TR, SP Railway Station, to finish the ride. *78km (48.5 miles)*

Places of interest along the route

A Thetford

An ancient town at the confluence of the River Thet and Little Ouse River, at one time capital of East Anglia, and, more recently, used in the filming of *Dad's Army*. **Thetford Priory** was once the third largest priory in Norfolk. It was founded circa 1103 and a further chapel and tower were added during the 13th century. Free access at all reasonable times. The **Charles Burrell Museum** commemorates this manufacturer of steam engines and agricultural machinery, telling the story of the company, the employees and the engines. Open April to October, weekends and Bank Holidays 1000–1700; June to September also Tuesday 1015–1245. Charge. Telephone (01842) 751166. The **Ancient House** was built in the 15th century and today contains the Tourist Information Centre and a museum of local history. Open all year, Monday–Saturday 1000–1230 and 1300–1700, Sunday 1400–1700. Charge for museum only July and August. Telephone (01842) 752599. **Thetford Forest Park** is to the north west of the town, on the B1107. Although a working forest, there is a visitor centre and waymarked cycle trails. Cycle hire and refreshments available. Picnic areas. Vistor centre open Easter to October, daily 1000–1700. Telephone (01842) 815434. For more information see also www.thetford.org.uk

B Banham Zoo, Banham

The zoo has plenty for visitors to see and do, with over 1000 animals in 14ha (35 acres) of landscaped parkland. Also gift and craft shops, pub, restaurant and coffee shop. Open all year, daily from 1000; summer last admission 1630; winter last admission 1500. Charge. Telephone (01953) 887771; www.banham-zoo.co.uk

C Diss

The town's name is said to come from the Anglo-Saxon *dic*, which means standing water – Diss is on the River Waveney and surrounds a 2.5 ha (6 acre) lake, the Mere. **Diss Museum** is located in the old Shambles building and has changing displays on the local history. Open all year, Wednesday and Thursday 1400–1600, Friday and Saturday 1030–1630. Charge. Telephone (01379) 650618.

D Bressingham Steam Museum and Gardens, near Diss

The steam museum features mainline locomotives, small stationary engines and traction engines, including a Victorian steam roundabout. There are three narrow gauge railway rides running around the gardens, woods, meadows and lakes. Visitors can also see Foggy Bottom, the plantsman Alan Bloom's garden. Also plant centre. Refreshments available. Open Easter to November, daily. Telephone (01379) 687386 to confirm times.

Food and drink

Plenty of choice in Thetford and Diss. The route passes several pubs and there is a post office/store in Croxton and in Kenninghall. Refreshments are also available at Banham Zoo and Bressingham Steam Museum and Gardens.

Route information

Distance   88.5km (55 miles)

Grade   Moderate

Terrain   Mostly flat, quiet roads, with gentle climbs at the start and finish of the ride. A few short stretches along A and B roads.

Time to allow   5–7 hours.

Getting there by car   Norwich is at the junction of the A47 and A11 and can also be reached via the A140 and A146. Follow SP Railway Station and park in the multi-storey car park facing the railway station (the start of the route) on Riverside Road.

Getting there by train   This route can be started from Norwich or Beccles railway stations. See page 13 for travel information.

Norwich is a cycle-friendly city and this route follows sections of the National Cycle Network (NCR 1) out of the city. From Norwich the route goes south west, follows a short section of NCR 1, crosses the River Yare by ferry and continues across the Norfolk/Suffolk border to Beccles. From here the route turns north east and returns to Norwich, following NCR 1 for much of the way. As an alternative, the route can be started from either Norwich or Beccles Stations and ridden as a one-way route, returning to the start by train. The chain ferry across the River Yare takes a couple of minutes and

fares are taken aboard the ferry. It operates all year, daily 0730–2200. Telephone (01493) 700429 for more information.

Route description

If starting from Beccles railway station, leave station and SO into Station Road. TL at XR and follow one-way system, SP Town Centre. TR at TJ into Blyburgate, SP Town Centre. TR into Hungate then TR at TJ, joining NCR 1. Following SP NCR 1, TL into Saltgate and continue SO as road becomes Northgate. TL at XR, SP Gillingham/NCR 1. Cross River Waveney and TL, SP Geldeston/NCR 1. Start route from direction 31.

If starting from multi-storey car park in Norwich, TL into Riverside Road. Continue SO at next two XR.

From Norwich railway station, exit via one-way system to Riverside Road, where TR. Continue SO at next two XR (SP cycle route to city centre at second XR).

1   Take second exit at roundabout into Gurney Road, SP Mousehold Heath. Continue to XR with A1402.

2   SO at XR into Salhouse Road. SO at next XR, following Salhouse Road as far as Sole and Heel pub.

3   TR, SP Great Plumstead.

4   SO over railway crossing. SO at next XR, SP Great Plumstead.

5   TL, SP Little Plumstead (8km/5 miles). Continue along this road and take RHF. Then TL at TJ, SP Little Plumstead.

6 SO, SP Blofield. Continue along this road, past lane on LHS and Blofield Hall on RHS.

7 SO, SP Hemblington.

8 TR at TJ, SP Blofield. Continue SO past Field Lane on LHS.

9 TL into Bullacebush Lane, SP Hemblington. TR into Plantation Road, SP Blofield. Continue SO, SP Norwich/Blofield and cross A47. Cycle through Blofield and continue SO.

10 TL into Doctors Road. SO at XR into Danesblower Lane and TR to stay on Danesblower Lane.

11 TL at TJ into Pound Lane.

12 TL at TJ, then TR.   *16km (10 miles)*

13 TR at TJ. Immediately TL then TR into Low Road, SP RSPB. Continue along this road, past Strumpshaw Fen.

14 TR at TJ. SO across level crossing. Continue along lane (no vehicle access) to Buckenham railway station, where TR across railway.

15 TR at TJ, SP Beighton. Continue SO past isolated barn and service road.

16 TR into Carrs Road. SO at XR, SP Cantley.

17 LHF, to avoid uneven bridleway. TR at XR, SP Cantley, and continue SO, passing bridleway on RHS.

18 TL at XR, SP Cantley (24km/15 miles). Pass village SP. SO at XR, SP Limpenhoe.

19 TR at TJ into Church Road, SP Reedham. Take LHF and pass church. Then RHF and LHF and continue SO.

20 TR at TJ and continue SO, SP Reedham.

21 TR at TJ, SP Reedham. Continue along this road, following SP Reedham. Pass Reedham Station and main road into village.

22 SO, SP Ferry. Catch ferry across river and continue SO.

23 LHF, SP Thurlton (32km/20 miles). Continue SO towards Thurlton.

24 TL at staggered XR, SP Gillingham. Take RHF, passing Queens Head pub then village SP on LHS.

25 TR into Sandy Lane. TL into North Farm Lane.

26 Arrive XR with B1136 and SO into The Spinney (road name).

27 SO at staggered XR, SP Beccles. Then TR at TJ onto B1140, SP Gillingham.

28 SO, past lane to Toft Monks (40km/25 miles). SO at next XR.

29 TR (CARE) at TJ onto A143. Look for white railing of footpath leading to lane and TL to follow footpath into lane. Continue SO, past lane on RHS and church on LHS, and TR towards A146. TR at TJ (CARE) onto A146.

30 To visit Beccles or to return to Beccles Station, TL and follow SP NCR 1 into town.

Otherwise, to continue route, TR, SP Gillingham.

31 TL into Kings Dam Road, SP NCR 1.
        48km (30 miles)

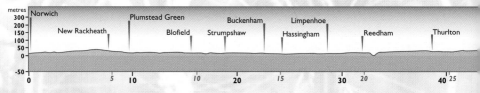

32 TL at TJ, SP Geldeston/NCR 1. Continue SO, past Heath Road on RHS, then post office, pub and village SP.

33 TL at XR, SP Ellingham/NCR 1. Continue SO, past former railway station on RHS.

34 SO, past Braces Lane on RHS. Then SO, SP Ditchingham/NCR 1. Cross bridge over dismantled railway line. Continue, following road past primary school.

35 SO (CARE) at XR with A143 into Wardley Hill Road, SP NCR 1.

36 TL at XR, SP Broome/NCR 1. Continue to complex five-way junction.

37 TL then TR and TR again, SP Loddon Ingloss/NCR 1.   *56km (35 miles)*

38 TR at TJ, SP Loddon/NCR 1. SO, passing lanes on RHS and LHS. Then SO at staggered XR, SP Chedgrave/NCR 1, and continue into Loddon.

39 TL at TJ, SP Chedgrave/NCR 1. Take RHF into Langley Road, SP NCR 1. SO at XR, SP NCR 1, past Chedgrave village SP.

40 TR, SP Hardley/NCR 1. SO at XR, SP Langley/NCR 1.

41 TL at TJ, SP Claxton/NCR 1. Pass pub and war memorial.

42 RHF, SP Claxton/NCR 1.

43 SO, SP Claxton/NCR 1. Pass village hall and continue SO, following SP Rockland/NCR 1 (72.5km/45 miles). Arrive Rockland St Mary.

44 SO past New Inn pub, and stay on this road, ignoring lane on RHS.

45 TR, SP Surlingham/NCR 1. Continue SO, SP NCR 1. Pass Holloway Road on LHS.

46 LHF, SP Bramerton/NCR 1. Continue SO, ignoring lanes on RHS, following SP Bramerton.

47 LHF, SP Bramerton. Continue SO, following SP Bramerton.

48 TR, SP Woodend/NCR 1. Continue SO, past Hill House Road on RHS. Follow road as it descends to and then climbs away from river. Pass farm buildings on RHS.

49 TR onto bridleway, SP NCR 1 (80.5km/50 miles). Take RHF and follow well-defined bridleway as far as gate and concrete road.

50 TR onto concrete road (serves water treatment works) and continue SO, past Anglia Water Whitlingham Gate 1.

51 TR, SP NCR 1. Pass Whitlingham Barn and follow road under A47 and into Whitlingham Country Park (BEWARE of heavy vehicles – the country park is under development and there is still some commercial mineral extraction taking place). Continue SO, passing series of cattle grids, rowing club on RHS, ski centre on LHS.

52 TR at TJ, SP NCR 1. Pass Trowse village SP and cross river and railway to roundabout.

53 Join cycle path and take third exit at roundabout, SP Football Ground/NCR 1. TR at TJ, rejoining traffic, SP NCR. Follow King Street.

54 TR (leaving NCR 1), SP Football Ground. Cross swing bridge into Carrow Road (Koblence Avenue). TL into Wherry Road and arrive at TJ with Riverside Road. Follow SP back to car park or dismount and cross road to finish the ride at the railway station.

88.5km (55 miles)

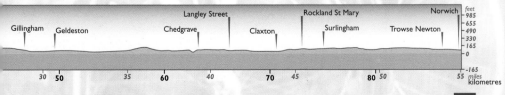

Places of interest along the route

A Norwich

Norwich is the county town of Norfolk and lies at the confluence of the Rivers Wensum and Yare. During the Middle Ages Norwich became the second richest city in the country through export of textiles. The medieval streets and buildings are well preserved, including sections of the city wall. Building on **Norwich Cathedral** started in 1096. The tower is a local landmark, standing 96m (315 feet) high. Open all year, daily 0730–1800. Guided tours available, June to October, Monday–Saturday. Free admission (donation requested). The **castle** was constructed in the 12th century and today contains the Royal Norfolk Regimental Museum and an art gallery. Guided tours available. Open all year, Monday–Saturday 1000–1700, Sunday 1400–1700. Charge. There is much else for the visitor to see in Norwich, including several museums and churches, and Coleman's Mustard Shop. Contact the Tourist Information Centre for more information (see page 13).

Norwich Cathedral

B Strumpshaw Fen

In the heart of the Norfolk Broads, the RSPB's Strumpshaw Fen has several nature trails through reedbeds, woodland and meadows, and birdwatching hides. Guided walks available. Picnic areas. Open all year, daily dawn–dusk. Charge. Telephone (01603) 715191; www.rspb.org.uk

C Beccles

A charming market town on the River Waveney, Beccles was once a Saxon seaport. Pleasure boats and small craft still pass the town and the quay is a popular place with visitors, and the start of a riverside walk. **Beccles Museum** is housed in the 17th-century Leman House, and contains displays on the history of the town and the surrounding area. Open April to October, daily (except Monday) 1430–1700. Admission free (donations requested). Telephone (01502) 715722.

Food and drink

Plenty of choice in Norwich and Beccles. Several pubs are passed en route.

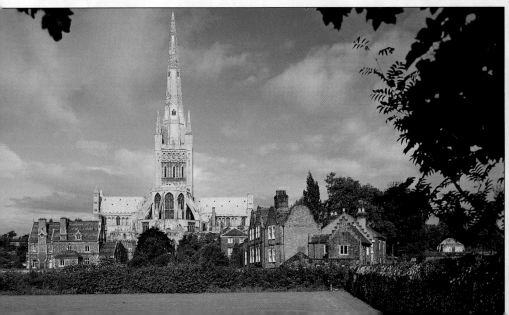

BRAMFORD, LAVENHAM AND THE STOUR VALLEY

Route information

Distance 99.5km (62 miles)

Grade Moderate

Terrain Undulating, quiet lanes, suitable for the moderately fit, riding bicycles with gears.

Time to allow 4–7 hours.

Getting there by car Bramford is 4.5km (3 miles) west of Ipswich, on the B1113 and B1067. There is a car park in the village. The route can also be started from Ipswich town centre by following directions from the railway station to the start of the route.

Getting there by train The nearest railway station is in Ipswich. See page 13 for travel information.

This route takes in some of the picturesque towns and villages around the Stour Valley in south west Suffolk. The route crosses several fords which may contain water depending on the time of year, although there is generally a walkway close by. From Bramford the route heads north and west through Kersey and Monks Eleigh to Lavenham. From here the route heads south to Boxford and Bures before returning to Bramford via Nayland and Stoke-by-Nayland. An alternative route reduces the total distance to 82km (51 miles) and bypasses Bures, Nayland and Stoke-by-Nayland.

Route description

If starting route from Ipswich railway station, TL out of station. Continue SO, through three sets of traffic lights and roundabout, and out of town. TR into Church Lane, SP No Through Road. Continue under A14 and TL at church. Continue route at direction 1.

From Bramford car park, cross river and TL into Fitzgerald Road. TL at TJ towards Sproughton.

1 TR by Wildman pub, SP Burstal. Then TR at TJ, SP Flowton.

2 TR, SP The Channel, and continue through village. TL at next TJ, SP Flowton Church. TR at Flowton Church, SP Somersham.

6.5km (4 miles)

3 TL, SP Elmsett. SO at foot of hill, SP Offton. Then TL at TJ, SP Offton.

4 TL by Limeburners pub, SP Offton. Take first TR, no SP but by speed de-restriction SP. Continue to TJ with B1078. *12.5km (8 mile)*

5 TL onto B1078 for approximately 3km (2 miles) and take second TL, SP Naughton. Pass Wheelhouse pub. TR to TJ, SP Semer. Then TR, SP Byroad (Rectory Road). Continue along this road and through ford.

6 TL (after ford), no SP. TL at TJ onto B1115 and take second TR, SP Kersey. Pass church and TR, SP Kersey. Pass through Kersey and take second TL, SP Bildeston.

7 TL, no SP. At Lindsey TL then TR, SP Monks Eleigh. TL onto A1141. TR by Monks

Eleigh green and village SP. Pass church and TR at TJ, SP Preston. **33.5km (21 miles)**

8 TL, SP Lavenham, and follow SP into Lavenham (41km/25.5 miles). Leave Lavenham on B1071 and continue into Washmere Green.

9 TL at XR, SP Byroad. TR at TJ, SP Little Waldingfield, and TL, SP Edwardstone. Pass church. **48km (30 miles)**

10 Follow SP Edwardstone. After Edwardstone, TR at War Memorial. Follow SP into Boxford.

11 TL in Boxford to join A1071. TR, SP Calais Street. Then TR on bend, no SP.
56km (35 miles)

12 To take shorter alternative route, arrive Calais Street and SO at bend, SP White Street. TR at TJ, past Polstead church. Take second TL, SP Scotland Street and continue to direction 14 where TL.

Otherwise, to continue main route, continue through ford to TJ and TL up hill, no SP. Take first TR, SP Assington. TR onto A134. Then take first TL, SP Assington. Continue through village and follow SP into Bures. TL onto B1508. TL by Bures Church, SP Nayland.
66.5km (41.5 mile)

13 Continue along this road into Nayland. Cross A134 onto B1087 and continue into Stoke-by-Nayland, where SO at XR, SP Hadleigh. TL at top of hill. **79.5km (49.5 miles)**

14 Continue along this road and take second TR, SP Shelley. TR at TJ, SP Higham. Again, TR at TJ, SP Higham. Take first TL, SP

Holton St Mary, then TL, SP Noakes Road. Continue to TJ with B1070 and TL, SP Hadleigh. TR on bend, SP Hintlesham. Continue to TJ.
87km (54 miles)

15 TR at TJ, SP Chattisham. Continue through village at TR at top of hill, SP Washbrook. Continue to junction where TL, SP Sproughton. Take second exit at roundabout onto B1113. Continue along B1113 and TR into Fitzgerald Road. TR at TJ, cross river to picnic site and retrace route back to Bramford to finish the ride. **99.5km (62 miles)**

Food and drink

There is a convenience store and fish and chip shop in Bramford. Plenty of choice in Lavenham and several pubs are passed along the way.

☕ **Corn Craft, Monks Eleigh**
Tearoom and craft shop. Open daily, all year.

Places of interest along the route

Ⓐ **Lavenham**
Lavenham is a former wool town, with many half-timbered buildings. See route 15 for more information.

Ⓑ **Heraldic Garden, Boxford**
Founded by Sir Conrad Swan, Garter Principal

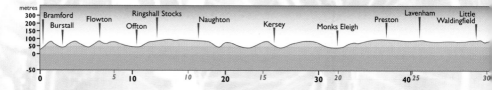

King of Arms, the garden incorporates the Lady Hilda Memorial Arboretum. Visitors are given an illustrated talk on the significance of heraldry, followed by a guided tour of the heraldic garden. Open by appointment only, June to August, daily. Charge. Telephone (01787) 210208.

Ⓒ Stoke by Nayland

A pretty village, dominated by the 36.5m (120 feet) high church tower. The church, much painted by Constable, is known for its font, brasses and tomb. Open all year, daily 0900–1700.

Stoke by Nayland

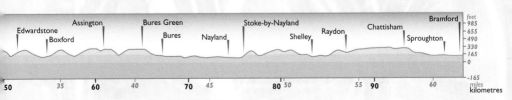

WELLS-NEXT-THE SEA AND FAKENHAM

Route information

 Distance   101km (63 miles)

 Grade   Strenuous

Terrain   Quiet lanes and stretches of off-road track with some rough surfaces and moderate climbs. There are short stretches of busier A and B roads.

 Time to allow   10–15 hours.

Getting there by car   Wells-next-the-Sea is is 14.5km (9 miles) north of Fakenham on the A149. There is plenty of parking in town, but use the car park at The Buttlands which is open 24 hours.

Getting there by train   There is no practical railway access to this route.

A route around north Norfolk. From Wells-next-the-Sea the route heads west to Heacham. From here the route turns south and east to Fakenham and then back to Wells-next-the-Sea. The route uses sections of the National Cycle Network (NCR 1) and the Peddars Way.

Route description

Leave The Buttlands and TL into Station Road.

1   TR into High Street. SO at XR into Church Plain. Then TR at TJ into Burnt Street. TL into Market Lane. Pass Alderman Peel High School and LHF onto unsurfaced section of Market Lane for gentle climb. Continue SO as track widens and meets farm track on LHS. Pass farm buildings on L and track on R.

2   RHF (as three tracks meet) joining NCR 1. SO at XR, SP New Holkham/NCR 1. Then SO at XR, SP Creake/NCR 1. SO at next XR, SO King's Lynn. Pass business entrance to Holkham Estate. Continue SO, past lanes on both sides and follow SP NCR 1 through Burnham Thorpe.

3   TR at TJ, SP Burnham Market/NCR 1 (9km/5.5 miles). SO at staggered XR, SP NCR 1. Continue to TJ where TL, SP NCR 1. Then TR, SP NCR 1, and climb Chalk Hill.

4   SO at XR (Sussex Farm on RHS). Continue SO, SP Ringstead/NCR 1. RHF at gates of Coseley Farm, SP NCR 1.

5   TL, SP NCR 1 (19km/12 miles). Continue SO, past lanes on L and R and Courtyard Farm. SO at XR, SP NCR 1.

6   To visit Gin Trap Inn, TR at TJ.

Otherwise, to continue route, TL at TJ, then SO past Hall Lane on RHS. TR, SP Heacham, leaving NCR 1. TL into Ringstead Road and

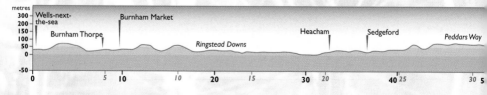

descend to XR with A149. SO at XR (staggered) and follow narrow lane down and across hump back bridge.

7 TR at TJ towards Heacham (26.5km/16.5 miles). Pass lane then pubs on LHS. SO at XR and follow SP North Beach. Cross bridge and follow unsurfaced road to roundabout.

8 TL at roundabout and follow sandy lane to South Beach. ***32km (20 miles)***

9 Arrive roundabout and TL across bridge to surfaced lane. TL at TJ, SP North Beach. Take RHF, SP North Beach.

10 TL at TJ, SP King's Lynn. SO at XR. Pass pubs on RHS. SO at XR (staggered), SP Fakenham/B1454. Pass entrance to Norfolk Lavender. Continue through Sedgeford and SO, SP Fakenham, as NCR 1 joins on R.

11 RHF, SP Fring. Pass war memorial on LHS.

12 TR at XR, SP Peddars Way, and join rutted grass track uphill. SO at next three XR, SP Peddars Way. Pass tracks on R and L then SO at next five XR, following SP Peddars Way, eventually joining surfaced road for descent to A148.

13 SO (CARE) at XR with A148 (49.5km/31 miles), following path to L of boarding kennels. Continue SO past farm buildings and tracks on RHS.

14 LHF at staggered XR onto surfaced road. Take RHF and continue SO into Great Massingham.

15 TR, pass pond and cross village green towards church. Take RHF and pass Rose & Crown pub on LHS. SO at XR, pass village SP and pond, and take LHF away from pond. TL at TJ and continue SO, past Sandy Lane and pond.

16 LHF, SP Weasenham (54.5km/34 miles). Continue to XR, where SO, SP Weasenham. SO at staggered XR, SP Wellingham. Continue into Weasenham St Peter and follow SP Wellingham through village.

17 TL at TJ onto A1065, SP Cromer. Pass pub and church.

18 TL into Low Street, SP Helhoughton. Continue to junction (airfield visible on LHS) and TR. Continue along this road towards West Raynham.

19 TL at TJ then take LHF and pass village SP. SO into The Street West and follow SP Helhoughton into village. TR at TJ, SP Hempton, and continue along this road, following SP Toftrees.

20 TL at XR, SP Shereford (46.5km/29 miles). SO at next XR, SP Shereford. Follow lane as it bends sharp R past church. SO at XR, SP Fakenham.

21 Arrive staggered XR with A1065 where SO.

22 TL at XR, SP Fakenham/NCR 1. Follow road towards Fakenham.

23 TL, SP NCR 1, and cross River Wensum. Take LHF (opposite Wensum Lodge Hotel) onto dedicated cycle path (80.5km/50 miles). Continue SO into Tunns Street. Take LHF into Quaker Lane, SP NCR 1.

24 To visit Fakenham for refreshment, TR at XR.

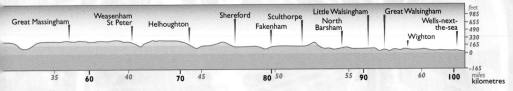

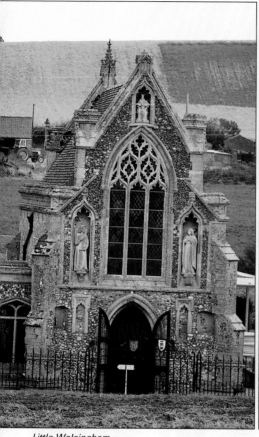

Little Walsingham

Otherwise, to continue route, TL at XR into Hall Staithe, SP NCR 1. Continue SO to end of cycleway (Sustrans Millennium Milepost here).

25 TR at TJ onto surfaced road. Continue SO, SP Walsingham/NCR 1.

26 TL at XR into Sculthorpe Road (staying on NCR 1). SO at XR with A1065, SP NCR 1 (use cycle/pedestrian crossing). Follow towards Sculthorpe. SO at junction with A148, SP NCR 1, into Creake Road (use cycle/pedestrian crossing). Follow this road, past two lanes on LHS and church. SO at XR with B1355, SP NCR 1. SO at next XR onto unsurfaced road, SP NCR 1.

27 TL at TJ onto surfaced road, SP NCR 1. TL at next TJ, SP NCR 1. Then TR at TJ, SP Walsingham/NCR 1.

28 TR, SP Walsingham/NCR 1 (88.5km/ 55 miles). Continue SO, between parapets of old railway bridge and past the Slipper Chapel. SO at XR towards Walsingham.

29 TL at TJ, SP Walsingham/NCR 1. Continue to XR where SO into Walsingham High Street then SO into Bridewell Street.

30 TR at TJ into Guild Street, SP Wighton/NCR 1. TL at TJ, SP Wighton/NCR 1 and pass war memorial on RHS.

31 TR at XR into St Peter's Road, SP NCR 1. Follow road past church and war memorial on LHS and cross River Stiffkey via ford. Continue up hill.

32 TL at TJ. Pass Great Walsingham's village SP and take second TL, SP NCR 1.

33 TL at TJ, SP Wells/NCR 1. Continue SO past lane and pub on RHS, chapel on LHS, lane on RHS.

34 TR at TJ, SP Wells/NCR 1.

95.5km (59.5 miles)

35 TL onto unsurfaced road, SP Byroad/ NCR 1, and follow road across railway line.

36 RHF then LHF into Market Lane. Pass track on LHS and farm buildings on RHS.

37 LHF and descend to surfaced road.

38 TR at TJ. Pass Alderman Peel High School on RHS. TR at TJ into Burnt Street.

39 TL into Church Plain. SO at XR into High Street.

40 TL at TJ into Station Road.

41 TL into The Buttlands and finish the ride.

101km (63 miles)

Food and drink

There is plenty of choice in Wells-next-the-Sea, Heacham and Fakenham. Various pubs are passed along the route and refreshments are available at Norfolk Lavender.

Gin Trap Inn, Ringstead
A varied menu available. The pub has an interesting collection of rural memorabilia.

Places of interest along the route

A Wells-next-the-Sea
The town is an ancient seaport and still supports a small fishing fleet as well as being popular with local sailors. The harbour area is a pleasant mix of old and new and there is a sandy beach, backed by dunes and pinewoods. Close by, on the A149 towards Stiffkey is the Wells and Walsingham Steam Railway which operates trains to Warham St Mary and Wighton between Easter and September. To the west of the town is Holkham Hall, built in the 18th century. Visitors can tour the house and gardens. Open June to September, Monday–Thursday and Sunday 1300–1700. Charge.

B Burnham Thorpe
The village rectory was the birthplace of Lord Nelson. Although the house no longer stands, All Saints Church contains many mementos of Nelson.

C Norfolk Lavender, near Heacham
Norfolk Lavender is in the grounds of an old watermill, Caley Mill. Visitors can enjoy the herb, rose and riverside gardens, and tour the lavender fields (May to September). Gift shop, plant sales and café. Open all year, daily 1000–1700. Admission free. Telephone (01485) 570384; www.norfolklavender.co.uk

D Walsingham
Walsingham comprises Great and Little Walsingham, once a popular place of pilgrimage. On the outskirts of the village is the Slipper Chapel, Shrine of Our Lady of Walsingham. The chapel was built in 1325 as the last wayside chapel for pilgrims approaching Walsingham and from here pilgrims walked bare foot into the village. The chapel is dedicated to Catherine, patron saint of pilgrims.

SUFFOLK – A GRANDE RANDONNÉE

Route information

 Distance 130km (81 miles)

 Grade Strenuous

 Terrain Mostly quiet country roads.

 Time to allow 7–14 hours.

 Getting there by car Bury St Edmunds is 37km (23 miles) north west of Ipswich on the A14, A143 and A134. Park in the Parkway open air car park, not in the adjacent multi-storey car park which closes at 1830.

 Getting there by train Bury St Edumunds railway station is on the London/Norwich line. See page 13 for travel information.

From Bury St Edmunds the route initially heads north west to Lackford and then turns north east up towards the Suffolk/Norfolk border, passing through West Stow, Thelnetham and Bressingham to arrive in Eye. From here the route drops down to Mickfield before turning east back to Bury St Edmunds.

Route description

Leave car park via pedestrian exit and TR into Chalk Road. Descend hill to join green cycle lane before junction with Risbygate Street. TL at TJ, joining cycle lane along Risbygate Street. Take first exit at roundabout (leaving cycle lane), SP Westerley.

1 Bear right, SP Westley.

2 SO, SP Little Saxham.

3 Take RHF, SP Barrow. Then SO, SP Barrow.

4 TR at XR, SP Risby.

5 TR at TJ (9km/5.5 miles) and continue to junction with A14. TR at TJ (CARE), then TL, SP Cavenham. Continue and take LHF, SP Cavenham.

6 TR at XR, SP Lackford.

7 TR at TJ to visit Lackford Wildfowl Reserve.

Otherwise, to continue route, TL at TJ, SP Mildenhall/A1101. *16km (10 miles)*

8 TR, SP West Stow. Continue SO, crossing Icknield Way and passing West Stow Country Park on RHS.

9 TL at TJ, SP Culford (village SP on RHS).

10 SO at TJ onto B1106, SP Culford.

11 LHF, SP Ingham. Then SO, SP Ingham, to reach XR with A134.

12 SO at XR, SP Great Livermere. *24km (15 miles)*

13 TL at TJ, SP Ampton. Continue along this road, passing Ampton Hall on RHS, St Peter's Church on LHS. Ignore roads joining from LHS.

14 TR at TJ, SP Thurston. Pass Great Livermore SP on LHS.

15 TL at TJ, SP Troston.

16 TL at TJ, SP Honnington.

17 Take RHF. **31.5km (19.5 miles)**

18 TR at TJ, SP Sapiston.

19 SO at XR. Then LHF to pass Honnington village SP on RHS.

20 LHF, SP Coney Weston. Pass Sapiston village SP on RHS.

21 SO at XR, SP Coney Weston. Continue SO, ignoring minor road on LHS, following SP Coney Weston.

22 TR at XR, SP Coney Weston.

23 LHF to join The Street, SP Hopton (40km/25 miles). Continue through Coney Weston and SO at XR, SP Hopton.

24 TR at TJ, SP Hopton.

25 SO at XR, SP Thelnetham.

26 To visit Thelnetham Windmill, TL at XR.

Otherwise, to continue route, SO at XR, SP Hinderclay. Then SO at next XR, SP Hinderclay.

27 TL at TJ into Fen Road, SP Redgrave.
48km (30 miles)

28 TL at TJ, SP Redgrave. SO at XR, SP Palgrave. Pass access to Bressingham Steam Museum and Gardens. Then TR following byroad, no SP.

29 TR at TJ. TR at next TJ, SP Mellis. Then, TL at TJ, SP Mellis. **57km (35.5 miles)**

30 TR at TJ to reach TJ with A143, where TL. Then TR (CARE), SP Purgate. Continue SO.

31 RHF, passing Dam Lane on LHS. Take LHF, SP Yaxley. Cross railway.

32 SO, SP Yaxley, and cross eastern edge of Mellis Green. Continue SO, following SP Yaxley/Heart of Suffolk Cycle Route (HSCR).

33 SO at XR, SP Yaxley/HSCR.

34 RHF and pass Cherry Tree pub and Yaxley village SP. TL, SP Eye (before post office). Arrive staggered XR with A140. Cross A140 (using cycle lane), SP Eye/HSCR (65km/40.5 miles). Continue SO, SP Eye/HSCR.

35 TR at TJ into Lambeth Street, SP Debenham. LHF then SO, pass war memorial and town hall on RHS. Join Broad Street and pass Kerrison Memorial on RHS.

36 TR, SP Stowmarket/B1117/HSCR/Magdalen Street.

37 TL, SP Braiseworth/HSCR. Follow lane as it passes between Rook Hall farmhouse and outbuildings. SO, SP Thorndon, and pass redundant church and lane leading to remote farms. Continue SO, SP HSCR.

38 TL at TJ, SP Thorndon/HSCR. SO at XR, SP Debenham/HSCR (72.5km/45 miles) and continue SO, following SP Debenham/HSCR.

39 TR by church, SP Wetheringsett/HSCR.

40 TR, SP Wetheringsett/HSCR, and continue along this road, past timber-framed farmhouse on RHS.

41 RHF, SP HSCR.

42 TL at staggered XR, SP Debenham/HSCR.

43 RHF, SP Brockford/HSCR. Then SO, SP HSCR.

44 RHF, SP Brockford. **80.5km (50 miles)**

45 TL at TJ, SP Mickfield.

Eriswell

Eriswell Low Warren

N

Lakenheath Warren

Parsonage Heath

THETFORD

Tutt Hill

Seven Hills

Rushford

Rushford Heath

A1066

Little Ouse River

Elveden

Thetford Heath

Barnham

Euston

Euston Park

22

Lodge Heath

Hall Heath

A11

West Calthorpe Heath

A1088

Little Fakenham

21

Berner's Heath

Culford Heath

Bowbeck

20

50

Sapiston

Honington

A1065

Icklingham

The King's Forest

Culfordheath

B1106

A134

19

18

Ixworth Thorpe

River Lark

A1101

Cavenham Heath

Icknield Way

17

14

Troston

16

Great Livermere

Ixworth

Tuddenham

8

West Stow

10

11

Ampton

12

†

Ampton Hall

15

Lackford

7

B

C

West Stow Country Park & Anglo Saxon Village

Ingham

13

Cavenham

9

A1101

Culford

A134

Timworth Green

A143

A1088

59

Lackford Wildfowl Reserve

6

Hengrave

B1106

B1106

Pakenham

61

50

Fornham All Saints

River Lark

Fornham St Martin

Great Barton

60

50

Risby

A14

B1106

A143

62

Higham

A14

A14

A1101

Thurston

Upper Green

Westley

A14

P

A

70

63

Barrow

5

69

A14

Blackthorpe

64

100

4

Great Saxham

3

Little Saxham

2

1

72

71

68

66

Rougham

Denham

Horringer

BURY ST EDMUNDS

67

65

Rougham Green

Hessett

Dunstall Green

Ickworth Park

Nowton

Hargrave Green

Chevington

A143

Hawstead

Bradfield St George

Hargrave

B1066

A134

Gedding

Chedburgh

Whepstead

100

Bradfield Combust

Bradfield St Clare

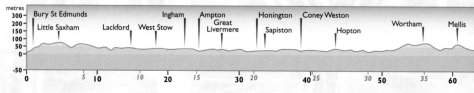

metres
300
200
150
100
50
0
-50

Bury St Edmunds

Little Saxham

Lackford

West Stow

Ingham

Ampton

Great Livermere

Honington

Sapiston

Coney Weston

Hopton

Wortham

Mellis

0   5   10   10   20   15   30   20   40 25   30 50   35   60

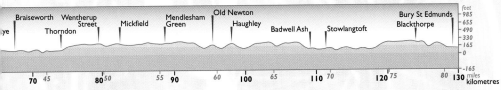

46 TR at XR, SP Old Newton/HSCR, and continue to XR with A140.

47 Cross A140 via cycle lane, SP Middlewood Green/HSCR. Then RHF, SP Stowupland/HSCR.

48 RHF, SP Cotton. Follow SP Mendlesham and then SP Gipping.

49 Take LHF to XR, where TL, SP Old Newton. Then RHF Old Newton. Continue along this road.

50 RHF, SP Old Newton. LHF, SP Haughley. Then SO, SP Haughley, passing St Mary's church then two lanes on LHS.

51 SO at XR, SP Haughley. Then LHF down towards Haughley and cross railway line.

52 TR at TJ into Old Street, SP Wetherden. Take RHF, passing Haughley village SP on RHS, pump on LHS.

53 TR, SP Wetherden. Continue SO, SP Wetherden, passing Jack's Lane on RHS.

54 LHF to XR, where TR, SP Uppertown. Then RHF and continue SO, SP Wyverstone.

55 TR at TJ, SP Wyverstone

105.5km (65.6 miles)

56 TL at TJ, SP Badwell Ash. Then SO, SP Badwell Ash.

57 TL at TJ, SP Pakenham. Pass St Mary's church on RHS. Continue SO, SP Stowlangtoft.

58 SO, SP Pakenham, past Stowlangtoft village SP and St George's church on RHS. Then RHF, SP Pakenham, and continue to XR with A1088.

59 SO at XR, SP Pakenham.

113.5km (70.5 miles)

60 SO, SP Great Barton. Pass post office on RHS. Then RHF, past village hall on RHS, pub on LHS.

61 TL at XR, SP Thurston. Take LHF, passing XR of unsurfaced bridleways, rugby club and school.

62 SO at XR, SP New Green. Descend hill, past Thurston railway station and pub on LHS.

63 TL at TJ, underneath railway arch, then take RHF. SO at XR, SP Rougham, and follow road across A14.

64 SO at XR, SP Rougham (120km/ 74.5 miles). TR, SP Bury St Edmunds. Pass St Mary's church and school on RHS.

65 TR at TJ, SP Bury St Edmunds.

66 SO, ignoring turnings to A14 and Blackthorpe Barn. Continue SO, SP Bury St Edmunds. Then LHF, SP Byroad.

67 Take RHF towards Rushbrooke, no SP.

68 TR, SP Bury St Edmunds.

69 TL at TJ and take first exit at roundabout, SP Town Centre/Bury St Edmunds. Look out on RHS for bridleway between river and overhead power lines (before service station). TR and join bridleway alongside River Lark towards abbey.

70 Bridleway meets paved cycleway. TR and follow cycleway into County Hall car park. SO at XR, around cycle calming chicane. Pass Court House and TR into tree-lined avenue towards museum. Take LHF, pass statue of St Edmund and between abbey and restored gate to face Chequer Square.

71 SO at staggered XR into Churchgate Street (one-way). TR at TJ into Guildhall Street. Then SO at TJ, join cycleway and TL into Woolhall Street, leaving one-way system. TR at TJ into St Andrews Street North. Look out for cycleway on LHS (before bus shelters, at start of cattle market car park).

72 TL to join cycle way and follow it through car park to crossing at Parkway South (light controlled). SO, via crossing. TR into Parkway car park and finish the ride.

130km (81 miles)

Bury St Edmunds

Ⓐ Bury St Edmunds

Bury St Edmunds is an old market town on the River Lark and retains many fine Georgian buildings. **St Edmunds Abbey** was one of the largest and most influential abbeys in medieval Europe. Today visitors can see the abbey ruins, the restored Abbey Gate and the gardens (tearoom open April to September). Open all year, daily. Free admission. The associated visitor centre explains the abbey's history. Open Easter to October, daily 10000–1700. Admission free. Telephone (01284) 763110. The **Manor House Museum**, Honey Hill, is housed in a Georgian mansion and displays collections of costume, art and horology. Tearoom. Open all year, Tuesday–Sunday and Bank Holiday Mondays 1200–1700. Charge. Telephone (01284) 757076. **Moyse's Hall Museum**, Cornhill, is housed in a Norman town house which has in the past been used as a tavern, gaol, police station and railway parcels office. The museum describes the local history of Bury St Edmunds and the surrounding area. Open all year, Monday–Saturday 10000–1700, Sunday 1400–1700. Charge. Telephone (01284) 757488; or visit www.stedmunds.co.uk and www. stedmundsbury.gov.uk

B **Lackford Wildfowl Reserve, near Lackford**
Restored gravel pits, home to wildfowl and wading birds. There are several hides. Free access at all reasonable times. For more information, contact Suffolk Wildlife Trust on (01473) 890089; www.wildlifetrust.org.uk

C **West Stow Country Park and Anglo-Saxon Village, West Stow**
The country park comprises 51ha (125 acres) of heathland, woodland and a large lake. Also visitor centre with café and shop and a reconstructed Anglo-Saxon settlement, built where an original settlement was excavated. Visitor centre, café and shop. Park open all year, daily 1000–1700 (closes 2000 in summer). Visitor centre and settlement open all year, daily 1000–1600. Telephone (01284) 728718.

D **Thelnetham Windmill, Thelnetham**
A 19th-century tower mill, worked by wind power. Open Easter, Monday Bank Holidays and Sundays (July to September), 1100–1900 Charge. Telephone (01473) 726996.

E **Bressingham Steam Museum and Gardens, near Diss**
A steam museum and plantsman's garden. See route 21 for more details.

F **Eye**
Eye is a historic market town. A town trail, available from the Tourist Information Centre, describes the local history and buildings. **Eye Castle** comprises Norman and medieval remains and offers excellent views of Eye (a good place for a picnic). Open Easter to September, daily 0900–1900, or dusk if earlier Charge. Eye Church is well-known for its beautiful stonework and a magnificent rood screen. Open daily all year, summer 0830–1800; winter 0830–1600.

Food and drink

There is plenty of choice in Bury St Edmunds and Eye. Several pubs are passed en route and most of the villages have a post office or a shop. Refreshments are also available at St Edmunds Abbey gardens, the Manor House Museum, West Stow Country Park and Bressingham Steam Museum and Gardens.

Q **Olde Tea Shoppe, Wortham**
In a picturesque setting. Meals and snacks served daily in summer; winter closed all day Sunday and Tuesday afternoons.

THE CTC
(Cyclists' Touring Club)

working for cycling

CTC is the UK's national cycling organisation. With seventy thousand members and affiliates, the club works for all twenty-two million cyclists in England, Wales, Scotland and Northern Ireland. CTC successfully lobbies on behalf of all cyclists and helped the government create its National Cycling Strategy. CTC also campaigns for improved countryside access, better cycling facilities on roads and at the workplace, and more space for bikes on public transport.

CTC provides essential services and invaluable advice for novice and experienced cyclists of all ages and abilities. It has 64 District Associations with 204 local groups plus hundreds of local campaigners in its Right to Ride network. New members and volunteers are always welcomed!

Cyclecover Insurance Services

CTC membership includes free third party insurance and legal aid. CTC also offers several cycling-specific insurance policies. Cyclecover Rescue is a unique twenty-four hour rescue scheme for cyclists stranded by breakdown (excluding punctures), accident, vandalism or theft. CTC offers annual travel insurance and single trip cover. Mountain biking, touring, repatriation of bike, luggage and accessory cover are all included. Comprehensive cycle insurance is offered to members and non-members alike, at very competitive premiums.

CycleSafe

Local authorities are being urged to sign up to four CycleSafe objectives, the aims of which are to improve safety for cyclists. That means reducing risks on roads, consideration for cyclists in new road layouts, adequate investment in cycling facilities and in cycling promotion. CTC has offered all authorities advice on engineering measures, education and examples of successful schemes elsewhere. In York, Britain's most cycling-friendly city, the implementation of a comfortable cycling environment has increased cycling by sixteen per cent and led to a ten per cent drop in cycling casualties in the last 20 years.

Technical and Touring Advice

CTC offers advice on buying a bike and other cycling equipment, maintenance and repair. CTC's events department has information on hundreds of routes both in the UK and abroad and experienced leaders run holidays to scores of destinations throughout the world. These tours are suitable for all cyclists ranging from families with young children to experienced distance riders.

CTC Magazine

Cycle Touring and Campaigning is CTC's bi-monthly magazine which is free to members. Articles cover campaign news, tours, technical advice, event reports and equipment tests.

CTC Help Desk

Staff on the Help Desk answer queries on all things cycling, from contacts at your local group to the best route across the continent. The Help Desk can advise on travelling by train or bus with your bike, bike security and parking facilities in public places and on how to make the workplace more friendly to cyclists.

CTC Membership

Membership costs from just £15 per year. Whether you are a roadster, prefer the quiet of canal paths and the countryside, commute by bike or just enjoy a day out with the children, CTC is the essential accessory for you!

For more information contact the CTC Help Desk:
CTC, 69 Meadrow, Godalming, Surrey GU7 3HS
Telephone (01483) 417217
Fax (01483) 426994
Email helpdesk@ctc.org.uk
Website www.ctc.org.uk

Cyclecover Travel Insurance
For a quote or instant cover call the CTC Help Desk or visit www.cyclecover.co.uk

Cyclecover Rescue
Telephone free on 0800 212810.

Cyclecover Cycle Insurance
Telephone free on 0800 169 5798.

CycleSafe
Visit www.cyclesafe.org.uk